Swami Dayananda is an outstanding scholar and teacher of Vedanta who is held in high esteem by the academic and traditional pundit alike. Having extensively studied the Upanishads, logic and Sanskrit grammar under the guidance of various teachers, his deep scholarship lends great clarity to his teaching. In addition, his style and vivid communication skills establish a remarkable rapport with his audiences, whether it be gatherings of several thousands which regularly attend his talks in India or seminars at universities all over the world.

Swami Dayananda has conducted several intensive teacher-training courses in the methodology of Vedanta at his ashrams in Rishikesh, India, and Pennsylvania, USA. Many of those trained by him are now in turn actively teaching Vedanta. Swami Dayananda himself travels indefatigably to all parts of the world, teaching and lecturing, unfolding the universal message of Indian philosophy.

INTRODUCTION TO VEDANTA

UNDERSTANDING THE FUNDAMENTAL PROBLEM

Swami Dayananda

Edited by
Barbara Thornton

VISION BOOKS

Also by Swami Dayananda

The Teaching of the Bhagavad Gita

www.visionbooksindia.com

First Published 1989
22nd Printing 2018

ISBN 81-7094-289-6
ISBN 13: 978-81-7094-289-4

Published by
Vision Books Pvt. Ltd.
(Incorporating Orient Paperbacks & CARING imprints)
24 Feroze Gandhi Road, Lajpat Nagar 3
New Delhi-110024, India.
Phone: (+91-11) 2984 0821 / 22
e-mail: visionbooks@gmail.com

Printed at
Anand Sons
C-88, Ganesh Nagar, Pandav Nagar Complex,
Delhi-110092, India.

Contents

III. The Informed Seeker

IV. Ignorance and Knowledge

V. The Teacher

Publisher's Note

Swami Dayananda Saraswati is a traditional teacher of Vedanta, the teaching of the Knowledge of Self found in the Upaniṣads at the end of the Veda. In addition to giving public talks, Swami Dayananda conducts comprehensive residential courses in Vedanta and Sanskrit from time to time, training other teachers to carry on the tradition of teaching. Swamiji teaches his courses in English but uses texts printed in the original Sanskrit. He introduces and defines, as needed, technical Sanskrit words, helpful in grasping the subject matter, and frequently redefines them until they become familiar. This book is based on the opening talks given by Swami Dayananda at the start of a 3-year course in November 1979, at Piercy, California. The first text studied at this course was *Tattvabodha,* a simple textbook of definitions, comprising an outline of Vedanta. Swamiji's introductory talks were aimed at helping the new students discover the nature of the fundamental human problem. Barbara Thornton compiled, abridged, and edited the talks. Laurel Elkjer, Mahadevan Embrathiry, Diane Piskulic and Ruth Greenfeld assisted in editorial review and proofreading.

CHAPTER ONE
Human Pursuits

The Four Categories of Human Effort

A human being sees himself as a deficient person. His constant, compulsive pursuits make his sense of inadequacy evident. To escape from this deficiency, he struggles for a large number of things in life which fall under four main headings:

dharma	ethics;
artha	securities;
kāma	pleasures;
mokṣa	liberation.

All four are collectively called *puruṣārtha* that which is longed for by human beings. These are the goals *puruṣa*, the human being, struggles for.

The four basic human pursuits can be subdivided into two sets. One set, the pursuit of security and pleasure, *artha* and *kāma*, is shared in common with other living beings; the other set, effort in accordance with ethics, *dharma*, and the pursuit of liberation, *mokṣa*, is peculiar to human beings. The second, the human set of pursuits, arises because a human being is a self-conscious person. A self-conscious being is a thinker, with the capacity to reach conclusions about himself. This capacity has made possible the universal human conclusion: I am a limited, deficient being who must struggle for certain things through which I hope to become complete.

The Endless Search for Security: *artha*

Artha, one of the two pursuits human beings share with other creatures, stands for all forms of security in life: wealth, power, influence, and fame. Every living being seeks security in some form appropriate to itself. Animals, birds, fish, insects — even plants and microbes — all seek security. Shelter is sought, food is hoarded, the dog buries its bone, the bee fills a comb with honey, the ant tunnels out a storehouse for grain. All creatures have a sense of insecurity. They, too, want to be secure. However, their attitude and behaviour are governed by a built-in program. Their sense of insecurity goes so far and no further; the animal's struggle for security is contained, it has an end. For them no endless brooding over security.

For the human being, on the other hand, there is no end to longing and struggle.

The endlessness of human struggle to fulfil the sense of want, can be seen by analysing experiences. If it is money I seek, no matter how much I accumulate it never seems enough. Irrespective of how much money I have, I do not feel secure. I may then seek security in power and influence, spending on the buying of power the very money which I had struggled to accumulate — not that money has no longer any value for me, but that I now attach a higher value to power. I am seeking security through power. The struggle for wealth, power, and fame is endless. All these are struggles for security, because I feel I am insecure.

Because I am a self-conscious being, I have the capacity to feel insecure; I accumulate assets but the accumulation fails to make me feel secure. The gain is never enough. I am always driven to seek more and different kinds of security in a futile effort to create a condition of security.

The Mercurial Nature of Pleasure: *kāma*

Kāma stands for the many forms of sensual pleasure. All creatures seek what is pleasurable — through whatever sense organs available to them. For non-human creatures the pursuit of pleasure is defined and controlled by instinct. They pursue what they are programmed to enjoy, directly and simply. Their enjoyment is not complicated by philosophy or self-judgement. A dog or a cat eats what tastes good until it is full, quite unconcerned by considerations of health or aesthetics. Enjoyment begins, ends, and is contained in the moment, in accordance with an instinctual programme.

Human pursuit of pleasures is more complex. Our desires are driven both by instinct and personal value systems. One's instinctual desires, as a living being, are complicated by the human ability to entertain wide-ranging, changeable personal desires. Every human being lives in a private, subjective world where one sees objects as desirable, undesirable, or neutral — neither desired nor undesired. When I examine my attitudes towards these objects, I find that what is desired by me is not desired by me at all times, or at all places; nor is what I desire necessarily desired by others. What is desired, changes. Time conditions desire; place conditions desire; individual values also condition desire.

Take the example of a "garage sale" where I sell off to others what I once considered valuable; it is now of no value to me but is still prized by others. In turn, what others consider worthless, I find valuable. In fact, sometimes what one has sold as junk, one may later again consider valuable, because circumstances or attitudes have changed. As time goes by, some of what I now prize will lose value for me and I shall be ready to hold a new garage sale.

These shifts in value which cause objects to be regarded as desirable, undesirable, or neutral, also occur and affect one's attitude towards people, ideas, ideologies, situations, and places. All are subject to becoming desirable or undesirable or neutral. Old cars, old houses, old furniture, even an old husband or a wife, go from one status to another. This interchange goes on all the time. Subjective values do not remain the same; when values change, likes and dislikes also change. Likes and dislikes dictate the pleasures one seeks just as they dictate what one rejects or avoids. Part of seeking pleasure is avoiding what causes displeasure.

Both animals and human beings struggle to obtain the pleasant and avoid the unpleasant. The difference is that the human struggle is not determined and limited by any set pattern but is dictated by fluctuating values. These ever-changing values keep one ever-struggling.

Human Choice Requires Special Standards

Because the struggle for security, *artha*, and pleasures, *kāma*, is not instinctually controlled but guided by changing personal values, it becomes necessary for the human society to have a set of standards which is independent of any individual's subjective values that determine his likes and dislikes.

Since I have the faculty of choice, I must have certain norms controlling my various actions, *karma*. Not being preprogrammed, for me the end cannot justify the means. I have a choice over both ends and means. Not only must the end chosen be permissible, but the means to gain that end must also conform to certain values. This special set of values controlling the individual choice of action is called ethics. The human struggle for security and pleasure, *artha* and *kāma*, must be in accordance with an ethical choice. Ethical standards guide one to the consideration of one's neighbours' needs. In choosing the means of achieving what I want to achieve, I must take into account my neighbours' needs, too. Indifferent to his needs, I cannot use my neighbour as an object to achieve my ends. I must value his needs as well as my own.

Animals Need No Ethics

For animals the question of ethics does not arise. They have little unprogrammed choice over action. Actions controlled by instincts, not subject to choice, create no ethical problems. Merit does not accrue to the vegetarian cow nor demerit to the tiger who eats the cow.

The human being with his faculty of choice on the other hand, must first choose the end he wishes to pursue and then the means to gain that end. We exercise our power to choose our ends, particularly in the western societies, in an endless permutation of variety: in food, dress, style of living, etc. "My thing!" proclaims this individuality. Then, too, in the West there seems to be a value attached to choice which is labelled "spontaneous", but which really is impulsive. It is good that there are many different means and ends to choose from; it makes for a colourful collage. However, impulsive choice, or the choice of means simply because they are easy and convenient, may result in trampling upon one's neighbour, destroying his security, and causing him pain.

Source of Ethics: Commonsense

One discovers the source of ethical values by observing how one wants others to behave with reference to oneself. Ethical values are based on commonsense appreciation of how one wants oneself to be treated.

I do not want others to use deception (or some other disagreeable means) to take away from me what I want; therefore non-deception becomes a value to observe with reference to others even as I pursue my ends. The ends and means I want (or do not want) others to choose because of the way such choices affect me establish a standard in me by which I judge the propriety of the goals and the means I choose myself — a standard which takes into consideration the impact of my choices upon others. Such values comprise commonsense ethics, which are recognized and confirmed scripturally in a more comprehensive ethical doctrine — religious in nature — called *dharma.*

Interpretation of Ethical Mandates

Commonsense ethics are the "do and don't" rules based on how one wants to be treated oneself. When this basis of ethics is seen, it becomes clear that there may be circumstances which justify interpreting or suspending a given standard.

I want you to speak truthfully to me and not tell me lies. This is the basis of the universal ethic "Speak the truth; do not lie". But consider the doctor in the case of a gravely ill patient whose recovery is uncertain, a patient whose state of mind is weak and depressed. If, in the doctor's opinion, full knowledge of the gravity of his condition may hurt the patient's chances of recovery, must the doctor follow this ethical mandate? Probably not. In such circumstances, speaking the truth is subject to interpretation, taking into consideration all the factors involved. Similarly, the ethic of non-injury does not prohibit the work of the surgeon's knife or the dentist's drill.

To be Ethical is to be Fully Human

It is not necessary to be religious to be ethical. The ethical standards which specify the right and wrong means of achieving security and pleasures are based on commonsense. An irreligious person can be completely ethical by commonsense standards. To be ethical is to be fully human — not controlled by mere instincts.

A human being with his highly developed, self-conscious mind has the capacity to make unprogrammed choices and to reflect upon the consequences of his choices. This capacity has given rise to ethical guidelines. To be fully human is to utilize these guidelines in the exercise of choice.

To "do wrong" morally also is to be human. Animals, so far as we know, cannot commit ethical mistakes. There seems to be no ethical category controlling the pursuit of *artha* and *kāma* for animals. None is required, because animals have no unprogrammed ethical choices. But a man can choose the wrong means to gain his ends. With a mind capable of rationalization, he can always abuse the freedom of choice given to him; he can ignore commonsense ethical standards. When he does so, he does not fulfil his role as a human being in society. Society establishes rules to prevent and alleviate the suffering such abuse of freedom of choice can cause others through criminal and civil laws.

What Religious Ethics Add

Sometimes one can be clever enough to abuse freedom without transgressing man-made laws or, at least, without being caught. At this point religious ethics enter the picture. One must learn to distinguish well between commonsense ethics and religious ethics. Religious ethics confirm commonsense ethics and add a few more.

Religious ethics generally say: you may deceive your fellow man, you may escape the hands of the law, but you really cannot get away from the results of your actions. The results will catch up with you in some way, sooner or later.

Religious ethics also usually enjoin special duties and impose additional prohibitions, based not just on common sense but on some religious tradition or scriptural revelation. It is not necessary to follow these special ethics to be a good citizen; commonsense ethics are good enough for that.

The Religious Ethics Called *Dharma*

The religious ethics called *dharma,* found in the Veda, confirm commonsense standards, specify further religious "do's and don'ts", and add the concept of *puṇya* and *pāpa* — results produced by good or bad actions, now or hereafter.

According to *dharma,* human action has an unseen result as well as an immediate tangible result. The unseen result of the action accrues in subtle form to the account of the "doer" of the action and, in time, will fructify, tangibly, for him as a "good" or "bad" experience — something pleasurable or painful. The subtle result of good action, *puṇya,* fructifies as pleasure; the subtle result of bad action, *pāpa,* fructifies as pain. *Pāpa* can be defined as sin. Sin is the choice of either a wrong goal or a wrong means in the pursuit of an acceptable goal. This choice will bring an undesired result; the very kind of result that the doer wanted to avoid in the first place. *Pāpa* is paid for in terms of undesirable experiences. The word *puṇya* has no good English equivalent. It indicates the result of a good action which is not seen, but which will bring later a desirable experience, something that is pleasing.

The Ranking of the Fourfold Struggle

Dharma occupies the first place in the four categories of human goals, because the pursuit of security, *artha*, and pleasures, *kāma*, needs to be governed by ethical standards. *Artha*, striving for security, comes second, because it is the foremost desire of everyone. Everyone is obedient under the doctor's scalpel precisely because everyone wants to live. Granted life, one then wants to be happy, to pursue pleasures, *kāma*. I want to live and live happily; and both pursuits, the struggle for security and the search for pleasure, must be governed by ethics.

The last category is the goal of liberation, *mokṣa*, ranked last because it becomes a direct pursuit only when one has realized the limitations inherent in the first three pursuits.

"Falling into Place": *mokṣa*

Mokṣa, like *dharma*, is a peculiarly human pursuit not shared by other creatures. Even among human beings, liberation is a conscious concern of only a few. These few recognize that what they want is not more security or more pleasure but freedom itself — freedom from all desires.

Everyone has some moments of freedom, moments when one seems to "fall into place". When I "fall into place", I am free. These fleeting moments of falling into place are experienced by all human beings. Sometimes music causes one to fall into place; at other times it may be the fulfilment of an intense desire, or the keen appreciation of something beautiful. That everything is in place is evidenced by not wanting anything to be different in the circumstances of the moment.

When I do not want anything to be different, I know that I have fallen into place with what is. I know fulfilment. I need make no change to become contented. I am, for the moment, free — from the need to struggle for some change in me or the circumstances. If I should fall into place permanently, requiring no more change in anything, my life would then be, fulfilled, the struggle over.

The pursuit of *mokṣa* is the direct pursuit of that freedom everyone has experienced for brief moments when everything has "fallen into place". How can that freedom be gained? What kind of bonds deny such freedom? Let us now explore these questions.

CHAPTER TWO

The Fundamental Problem

The Locus of Error

When you see something but do not recognize it for what it is, you can take the thing for something other than what it is. Failure to see an object for what it is leads to a mistake as to the nature of the object. If the object is totally unperceived, there is only ignorance, but no mistake. A totally unperceived, unknown object never becomes the locus of error concerning its nature.

For example: Seeing a dark shape beside the path, in the greyness of dusk, I fail to perceive that it is a tree stump. Concluding that the shape is a man lurking in the shadows I become alarmed and go in another direction. My perception of "something" beside the path gave me a locus of making a mistake. Because I saw something but failed to recognize it for the harmless thing it was, I had a *basis* for making a mistake about what was seen — a mistake that caused me to change my direction.

My short-sighted neighbour and his keen-eyed wife, travelling the same path a few minutes later had no problem. He could not see even the outline of the old stump; so he made no mistake about it. There was no *scope* for him to make a mistake about it; he had no perception of it; he did not know it was there. His keen-eyed wife saw it clearly for what it was. So both went along the path happily, one in total ignorance of the existence of the object, and the other in clear knowledge of its nature.

An animal has little chance to commit an error about itself because its consciousness of itself as an individual is very limited. It does not appear to have much capacity for critical awareness of itself, or others. The cow does not pine because she is unable to give as much milk as her sister in the next stall. The alley cat is not depressed because it wants to be a bulldog. The horse does not spend hours in the meadow trying to fly. Not having the kind of self-perception that allows it to compare and judge itself, an animal has no basis for making a major mistake about its nature. Thus, an animal seems to have no basic confusion about itself; it appears to be free from the multitude of complexes that bother human beings. But a human being does have the capacity to commit such an error. Highly conscious of himself, he has a locus in which to make a mistake about himself. If, in looking at himself, he does not recognize himself for what he is, he will make a judgement about himself that will be something other than what his self is.

The Self-Judgement of Inadequacy

It is clear that one judgement the human being makes about himself is: As I now am, I am an incomplete being; I am deficient, inadequate."

The evidence of this judgement is seen in the compulsiveness and constancy of the human pursuit of security and pleasure. As a conscious being aware of the right and wrong means of gaining these goals, one often disregards this knowledge, choosing less than ethical means. Even when the means are proper, the great importance of *artha* and *kāma* can be seen in everyone's intense preoccupation with their gain.

The gain of security and pleasures assumes such importance because it is through their gain that one hopes to escape from want, inadequacy, and incompleteness and become a free, adequate person. "I want to be a complete person. As I am, I am not complete", is the common experience of everyone. This urge to be complete stems from seeing oneself as apparently incomplete. The high degree of human capability for self-perception makes possible the human judgement of lack of completeness.

All struggles in life are expressions of the urge to be complete. The conclusion that I am an incomplete person either accurately reflects my nature, or is a mistake. This will have to be decided. If it reflects my true nature, there is no need to seek further knowledge about myself for the sake of changing my conclusion that I am incomplete. On the other hand, if it is an erroneous conclusion, then I need to know more about myself in order to discover the completeness that seems to be hidden from me. Whether I am complete or incomplete, must be determined. But until it is determined, the "fact" is that I see myself as an incomplete person.

The Attempt for Completeness through Change

In most situations I see myself as incomplete, not wholly adequate. Whatever the circumstances may be, I do not feel truly at home; something further is needed. And I try to achieve completeness by changing the situation. For example: A young man, happily married, with three young children, a good job, a comfortable home, and a generally pleasant prospect for the future, none the less felt uncomfortable about his situation. He did not feel adequate under the circumstances because he was not putting aside funds for the children's college education. The children would not have good prospects in life unless they were educated. Yet, the college costs escalated every year. The young man therefore decided to take a second job. The job brought in some money which he began to invest. He felt less worried about college expenses but grew concerned over his health. Perhaps the strain of two jobs was too much; he was always tired and noticed some shortness of breath. He began to eat a special diet and joined a gym programme to build up stamina. His energy increased and his health was better than ever; but a sense that he was still not "on top of things" remained. He had been investing his extra funds in slightly speculative stocks. The stock market now begun behaving erratically; perhaps the better thing would have been to go in for some kind of real estate investment. But then again the days of major tax advantage in real estate were gone. Taxes might go up. Perhaps tax-free municipal bonds would be the best answer, although the yield would be modest. In the meantime, he began to think that he must find some way to spend more time at home with his children. They were growing up and he rarely ever saw them; his wife complained that she too, never saw him. He wanted to be a more involved father and more companionable husband. He needed to find a way to lessen the load and spend more time at home. And so it went on. Doggedly, he continued to work to bring about a change in the circumstances which he hoped would allow him to feel adequate, complete — at home with himself.

If you look closely at the variety of changes you work to bring about in the situations in your life, you will find that you make changes so that you will feel adequate. My attempt to change the situation is really an attempt to change myself. I do not try to change the situation in which I am at home with myself. But when I see myself as inadequate, I add new things into my situation so that I may feel better; or, I may eliminate some aspects from the situation in order to be comfortable.

Personal Values Determine Types of Changes

The types of changes one attempts to bring about in a given situation are dependent upon one's personal value system. Personal values are made up of subjective values and ethical values. Subjective values come from one's temperament, conditioned by one's own array of experiences of pleasure and pain. For example, if I am of an active temperament I am likely to be drawn to active persuits which I find to be pleasant. My ethical standards also will affect the choice I make, in some cases causing me to choose a less-desirable option or to shun a more attractive opportunity. My ethical values are those guiding standards which take into consideration the likes and dislikes of others. I accept ethical guidelines either because I have not resisted their imposition upon me by society, culture, or some other authority, or because I see their value for myself. In either case, I follow them because, I feel that I shall be more fulfilled by doing so rather than being guided solely by my personal likes and dislikes. Thus, ethical standards are also connected with the desire to court what is pleasant and avoid what is unpleasant.

Attitude towards Change

There is no problem with change itself. Change cannot be avoided. Life is a process of constant change. What is being discussed is a certain kind of expectation centred on change. The changes being talked about are the changes one is driven to make for the sake of altering one's situation, expecting such change will make one more comfortable, more adequate, more complete.

Our topic is not simple, matter-of-fact changes, made simply because the given circumstances call for a change; nor is it the casual, incidental changes one makes for the sake of variety to which one attaches no importance. We are talking about changes towards which one has certain expectations linked with one's conclusions about oneself.

For example: Preparing and eating food is one of the ordinary, matter-of-fact actions (change comes through action) that takes place daily; to carry one's food into the garden to eat at a picnic table on a pleasant day is an incidental, casual change. There is no problem with such changes. They are not changes sought for the sake of a change in oneself but are natural or incidental to the situation. However, eating in order to be happier, to soothe one, to ease one's hurt feelings, to escape from the moment, to make one feel more adequate is a change sought through the action of eating. Food carried outside to the garden because one wants the setting to banish one's depression, lift one's spirits, make oneself feel more whole, is a change one sought through eating one's meal in different surroundings.

Most changes one seeks are not for the sake of the change, but for one's own sake. When I am comfortable I stop all compulsive change-seeking. Through most of my change-seeking I am actually interested in a change in myself. The change I really want is the one that will make me comfortable in any situation — so adequate, so complete that no situation will bother me. If I became so, situational change, for the sake of completeness, would not be necessary for me. Compulsive change-seeking centres on oneself alone — in the hope that through change one can become a non-deficient, adequate person.

Gain through Change Always Involves Loss

This compelling need to be free from the feeling of inadequacy is found in everyone. Every human being has the problem of feeling inadequate, deficient, incomplete, and therefore, he tries to rid himself of inadequacy. This attempt is a basic urge; and, the attempt, universally, is in the form of change through which one gains security, *artha,* or pleasures, *kāma.* However, any gain that comes as a result of effort is not absolute. Every gain of security through effort involves a concomitant loss. The gain obtained is always offset by the time and effort expended, by the responsibility assumed, by some other alternative possibility sacrificed.

For instance, when I buy a large, impressive, well-appointed house, the pleasure and security I gain, which contribute to my feeling of adequacy and comfort, are offset by the money spent, the debt incurred, the cleaning staff required, the responsibility of maintenance and protection assumed, all of which take away something from the feeling of adequacy and comfort which I sought in the buying of the house in the first place.

Any gain from change also always involves a loss. When one gains something there may be an initial release from a sense of inadequacy, but one then finds that the original problem still remains. By gaining or disposing of one thing or another, the problem of inadequacy is not solved. Adequacy, freedom from being incomplete, is the end I seek behind all my forced pursuit of security, *artha*; but no gain or disposal accomplishes that end.

One does not achieve freedom, or adequacy by gaining something or by giving up something else. An inadequate person remains inadequate even upon gaining the desired thing. An inadequate person enjoying the disposal of some unwanted thing still remains inadequate. So the human problem — that one seems to be an incomplete being — is never solved by seeking security through gain or disposal.

Fickle Pleasure

The pursuit of pleasure, *kāma,* for the sake of adequacy, is no more satisfactory than the pursuit of security.

The gain of pleasure rests upon the convergence of three constantly changing factors, never fully predictable, nor, ever under one's control. Moments of pleasure require availability of the object, availability of the appropriate, effective instrument for enjoying the object, and presence of the proper frame of mind for enjoyment of the object.

I may have a strong desire for a fresh ripe peach, but no peaches may be available. On the other hand, I buy some peaches but a sudden attack of hay fever prevents me from enjoying their fragrance or taste. The hay fever passes. I am about to take a bite when news arrives of an accident injuring someone dear to me. My interest in the peach vanishes. I no longer have any appetite.

Even in the presence of the object and the availability of the right instrument, enjoyment can be denied for want of the right attitude.

Pleasure is momentary, because any of its contributory factors can, and do, change. Of course, we do have moments of joy from time to time, but being dependent upon the alignment of three changing factors they last but a moment. The objects of enjoyment are limited, bound by time. In the very process of enjoyment some get expended, and all are subject to change, in the hands of time.

The instruments of enjoyment also are time-bound, limited, and not capable of consistent performance. And the mind, being what it is — whimsical, capricious — gets tired of what it once eagerly desired and sought. The mind can discover monotony in objects. Thus, trying to maintain a moment of pleasure is like throwing a saddle over three wild horses sitting astride all three, and being able to successfully guide them in one direction.

Recognition of the Fundamental Problem

From looking at one's own life experiences one can see that what really underlies all one's continual striving is the desire to become totally free from all deficiency, to become complete and wholly adequate in all situations. But, except for fleeting moments, one always seems to be inadequate. The fundamental human problem is to become adequate; the solution chosen is the gain of security and pleasures. The result is temporary release, if any, but not an end to the sense of inadequacy.

Neither security nor pleasure brings about an end to inadequacy. So if one looks at one's own struggles for security, *artha*, and pleasures, *kāma*, one finds that the sense of adequacy, of fulfilment, that one hopes to obtain through *artha* and *kāma* are gained only occasionally, and only momentarily. The struggle never ends.

The Analysis of Experience

In the *Muṇḍaka Upaniṣad* it is said:

parīkṣya lokān karmacitān brāhmaṇo
nirvedamāyānnāstyakṛtaḥ kṛtena

tadvijñānārtham sa gurumevābhigacchet
samitpāṇiḥ śrotriyaṁ brahmaniṣṭham
(I. ii. 12 *Muṇḍaka Upaniṣad*)

Having analysed the worldly experiences achieved through effort, a mature person gains dispassion, discerns that the uncreated (limitlessness) cannot be produced by action.

To know That (the uncreated limitlessness), he, with twigs in hand, should go to a teacher who is learned in the scriptures, and who is steadfast in the knowledge of himself.

The Upaniṣad says that when a mature person analyses his own life experiences to see what he has achieved through his effort, he gains dispassion towards the results of effort. The gain of dispassion means that he has understood the inability of the results of effort to solve the basic human problem. His worldly experiences involving changes achieved through effort have brought about no lasting solution to his sense of incompleteness. However, although the problem has not been solved by worldly experience, this realization is nevertheless useful because it forms the basis of the analysis that leads him to discover the nature of his real problem. A real solution to a problem cannot be sought until the problem is seen for what it is; all analysis depends upon data.

The personal experiences in one's own life form the data for the analysis that enables one to discover the fundamental human problem. The gain and analysis of experiences is very important. It is through analysing one's experiences that one becomes mature.

Through analysing my own experiences, my efforts and actions, my gains and losses, I find that I consistently see myself as an incomplete person. No matter how many desirable things I gain, no matter how many undesirable things I get rid of, I remain deficient. In spite of all my various pleasures and security, I am an unfulfilled, inadequate person. When I see my experiences in this light, I become mature.

Maturity is shown not by seeking *better* experiences but by discovering, through an analysis of experiences, the basic human problem: what one wants is to be non-deficient, adequate — and that experiences do not make one non-deficient, adequate.

Inadequacy is Centred on Oneself

Analysis of one's own experiences reveals that one cannot solve the human problem by the pursuit and attainment of things in the world; nor does one solve it by renouncing worldly things. Gain or loss is all that can happen through action: either you gain something that you do not have, or you get rid of something that you do have.

Through either gain or loss, the discovery is the same: I am still inadequate. With something gained, I do not become adequate; free from something abandoned, I do not become adequate. The discovery is made: inadequacy is something centred on me, not on the possession or dispossession of something. I am inadequate because I am inadequate; the inadequacy does not depend upon any factor other than myself. Neither *pravṛtti,* the positive pursuit of something, nor *nivṛtti,* the turning away from things, cures my inadequacy. One can very easily see this by analysing one's own as well as others' experiences.

A mature person, a *brāhmaṇaḥ* [1], then, is someone who, having analysed his own experiences, has discovered that the total adequacy he seeks, is not gained through effort. He knows that regardless of his experiences he finds himself to be an incomplete person at all times. He recognizes that what he really wants is a drastic change in himself, not a situational change. He wants some change that will make him

1. In the context here *brāhmaṇaḥ* simply means a mature person. a "mature" person is not the same as a "wise" person, the latter being someone who knows the truth of his own nature.

a non-deficient, completely adequate person. He sees, too that all the changes that he wants to bring about are only changes for the sake of helping him become an adequate person.

Insight into Adequacy: the Norm for Self-Judgement

Everyone wants to be free from self-centred inadequacy. Why doesn't one accept oneself as inadequate? We can only say that it is because there seems to be an insight of adequacy. I have some insight into what it is to be adequate; therefore, I cannot accept not being adequate. The insight of adequacy comes whenever I have an experience wherein there is freedom from being an inadequate, deficient person. And such experiences occur in the lives of everyone. Whenever one experiences a moment of pleasure or joy, one sees oneself as an adequate person for a while. Whether the moment of joy comes from a slapstick joke or subtle humour, the sudden discovery of something wondrous or the gain of a highly desired object, or a certain sensory pleasure — any time you experience a moment of joy, however momentary, you see yourself at that moment as a person not wanting in anything, a happy person. Everyone has these moments in life, howsoever few and far between. One has the experience of oneself as an adequate person — complete, full. That experience of not wanting in anything becomes the norm by which the experience of being wanting in something is judged, and is judged as something one does not care for. One cannot consider something as bad unless one knows what is good. There is no dissatisfaction if there is no norm for satisfaction. We do not lack such a norm for adequacy.

Everyone has the experience of an adequate self. That is why one strives to be adequate. One has insight, in terms of experience, of an adequate self, momentarily free from all limitations, all lurking imperfection.

Therefore one struggles for security, *artha*, and pleasure, *kāma*, through which one sometimes seems to be able to gain these experiential moments of adequacy. But the struggle is usually abortive, futile, unfruitful, and, when successful, the moment is brief — the experience of adequacy does not last.

The Direct Search for Freedom from Inadequacy

Mokṣa becomes relevant when one realizes that behind one's struggle for security, *artha*, and pleasures, *kāma*, is the basic human desire to be adequate, free from all incompleteness, and that no amount of security or pleasure achieves that goal. *Mokṣa* means freedom from inadequacy. When I appreciate that what I am really seeking is a solution for my inadequacy, a problem centred on myself, I become an open-eyed seeker who knows what he is looking for. In Sanskrit there is a very precise word for such a seeker: *mumukṣu*. A *mumukṣu* is one who desires freedom from all limitation. A *mumukṣu* knows that his pursuit of the first three *puruṣārtha,* the first three of the fourfold human goals, does not solve his problem. His ethically guided, dharmic pursuit of *artha* and *kāma* does not resolve his inadequacy. He is then ready to directly seek adequacy. This adequacy is called *mokṣa,* liberation, and since it is something seekers consider a thing to be "achieved", it is listed as the fourth human goal, the fourth *puruṣārtha,* although as we shall see later liberation is not an "achievement" in the usual sense of the word.

So when a mature person analyses his experiences, he discovers that behind his pursuit of security and pleasure is a basic desire to be free from all insufficiency, to be free from incompleteness itself, a basic desire which no amount of *artha* and *kāma* fulfils. This realization brings a certain dispassion, *nirveda,* towards security and pleasures. The mature person gains dispassion towards his former pursuits and is ready to seek liberation, *mokṣa,* directly.

CHAPTER THREE

The Informed Seeker

The Futile Solution

From the experiences of his own life, a mature thinker discovers that security and pleasure do not solve his basic problem — his desire to be adequate, free from all limitation — in spite of the pleasures he has enjoyed or the security he has obtained. Pleasures, which always depend upon the favorable alignment of changing factors, do not last; neither does one find lasting completeness in them. Security is bound by time, limited in nature; loss offsets gain. Security too does not last forever. The inadequate person, holding on to insecure things, does not become secure. The unfulfilled person, gathering up moments of pleasure, does not become complete. The never-ending pursuit of security and pleasures betrays the continuing sense of insecurity and incompleteness on the part of the pursuer. The mature persons here realise that the pursuit of adequacy through *artha*, *kāma*, is futile. Equally futile is the attempt to gain adequacy through the giving up of such pursuits. Inadequacy is not dependent on the presence or absence of things. It is centred on oneself.

The Experience of Adequacy

That I seek adequacy is the result of my judgement that I am inadequate. Such a judgement could not be possible unless I had some idea of what adequacy is like. My idea comes from experience, the experience of moments of adequacy — moments in which I required no change in me or the world.

When I am adequate at that moment, I seek no other thing. I am just myself, seeking nothing. I need nothing; I crave no change, either in the situation or in me.

Such experiences of joy — moments of happiness — are there in everyone's life. Joy and inadequacy cannot exist in me at the same moment. When I am joyful I am adequate — and it is an adequacy that cannot be furthered. Adequate is adequate. There isn't a *more* adequate. There is no *supra* adequacy — only adequate. Adequacy does not come in degrees. Anything other than adequacy is inadequacy.

Because there are moments in which I find myself adequate, I am not totally without the experience of adequacy. But most of my experiences seem to establish me as inadequate, which I find I cannot accept. I constantly reach for adequacy. The rare moments of sufficiency give me a standard by which to judge myself as insufficient the rest of the time.

Distinguishing Knowledge and Experience

How can the contradictory experiences of adequacy and inadequacy be reconciled? Here it is necessary to distinguish knowledge from experience.

Knowledge is the grasp of what is. Experience is the direct perceptual participation in an event.

Experience can lead to knowledge, but the impression of experience need not be knowledge. Experience has to be assimilated in terms of knowledge. This is so because one may experience something and still be ignorant of it. Experience is one thing; knowledge of what I have experienced is quite another. When I have knowledge it includes perception — it includes experience. But experience does not have to include knowledge. For knowledge, what is experienced must be known for what it is. Experience may or may not coincide with knowledge. Knowledge is something that can both contradict experience and resolve the seeming contradictions in experience.

Experience can lead to knowledge. Experience need not include or be knowledge. Experiences can be contradictory. Knowledge includes experience. Knowledge can contradict experience. Knowledge can also resolve the contradictions in experience. Knowledge cannot be contradicted.

Any given set of perceptual impressions gained from experience may or may not conform to knowledge. To qualify as knowledge they must pass the test of inquiry.

For instance, the experience in most parts of the world is that the sun rises each day in the eastern sky and travels to the west where it sets. In the polar regions, at a particular time of the year, the experience is that the sun travels in a circle; Sunrise and sunset are not experienced. Which set of experiences should be taken as real? Are both sets of experiences real? An analysis becomes necessary. An inquiry must be made, taking into account all available factors. The questions are: Is the experience of a sun that rises in the east and sets in the west fact or not? Is this observation true? What about the polar sun that can be seen travelling in a circle? How does this observation correspond with fact?

Experience 1:	The sun rises and sets
Experience 2:	The sun moves in a circle
Knowledge :	With respect to the earth the sun is stationary, neither rising nor setting nor moving in a circle

The sun appears to rise or set or move in a circle from the standpoint of a particular spot on an orbiting planet turning on its axis. After inquiry and analysis, the contradictions are resolved in a true understanding of the relationship of the earth to the sun. The sun, although apparently in motion, is stationary as it relates to the earth. The appreciation of this fact is knowledge. The experiences were only *mithyā*, apparent — something which appears to be but is not so. The sight of a rising or setting sun may be a beautiful experience; but in terms of knowledge it is an illusion. Experiences may contradict each other; knowledge encompasses and reconciles the contradictions.

Inquiry into the Nature of Oneself: *ātma-vicāra*

With regard to oneself there are two contradictory sets of experience. Most of the time, experientially, I find myself to be inadequate; and yet, there are moments when I find myself adequate, not wanting — full and complete.

The question, thus, arises: am I adequate or am I inadequate? There is experience to support either conclusion. Or, perhaps, I must conclude that I am occaisionally adequate and often inadequate; or that I am occasionally inadequate and largely adequate. If these are the conclusions, then I must reflect how I become inadequate if in fact, I am adequate; or, vice-versa. Such reflection requires inquiry.

The inquiry necessary to resolve the particular question of self-adequacy is called *ātma-vicāra*. Ātma means "I" or self, and *vicāra* is inquiry.

Self-inquiry, *ātma-vicāra*, is necessary, because I have two contradictory sets of experience about myself. My ceaseless pursuit of things in the hope they will make me adequate shows that I experience myself as inadequate. I usually have a sense of being deficient. From this continual sense of deficiency, I conclude that I am inadequate. But sometimes I do experience moments of adequacy. It is from such moments that I know what it is to be adequate. These occasional experiences of adequacy make any conclusion that I am inadequate premature. The issue must be kept open. An inquiry is necessary to resolve the contradiction. I must examine and analyse my experiences to see which validly reflect fact and which are illusory.

Analysis of the Search for Adequacy

When I examine my search for adequacy, I find that adequacy is not an object in relation to me. Inadequacy is centred on me. I am an inadequate being. I seek adequacy as myself. I do not seek adequacy to be other than myself; but, I seek it through other things — through security *artha,* and pleasures, *kāma,* because that is the only way I know of seeking adequacy. Ceaselessly I seek adequacy through *artha* and *kama* until, finally, I am able to see that these pursuits do not lead me to adequacy. I become mature. I recognize that what I seek is adequacy itself — an adequacy not produced by gain of security and pleasure. I become a *mumukṣu,* a direct seeker of adequacy.

When I recognize the nature of the human problem and understand that it cannot be solved by pursuit of *artha* and *kāma,* I seem to be in a helpless position. What is left for me to do? *Artha* and *kāma* are all I know and there seem to be only two things to do with them: *pravṛtti*, the pursuit of gain, and *nivṛtti*, the renunciation of gain, neither of which solves the problem of inadequacy. *Artha* and *kāma* do not work. Perhaps the solution has to be simply to accept inadequacy.

But when one explores the possibility of accepting inadequacy, no solution to the problem is found. One does not find it posible to accept inadequacy. The seeking of adequacy is not a cultivated desire. It is not a desire one acquires along the way, born of circumstances and conditioning. A cultivated desire can be abandoned, but a natural urge cannot be given up. The ambition to be an astronaut is an acquired desire that can be dropped later for any one of a variety of reasons. But natural urges such as the urge to breathe or the urge to eat can never be dropped; one can hold one's breath but the urge to breathe remains; one can refuse food but the urge to eat is still there.

The urge to be adequate is universal and is not in one's power to give up; nor can one accept inadequacy and be happy.

I cannot give up my urge to be adequate nor can I accept inadequacy. I see that behind all my pursuit of security and pleasures is the fundamental urge to be adquate and that these pursuits do not make me so. Neither pursuit nor the abandonment of pursuit makes me adequate. Seeing all this I become a *mumukṣu*, a direct seeker of freedom from inadequacy who seems to have no other means to achieve what he seeks.

The Nature of Achievement

Achievement in life falls under two categories. The first category, which we know very well, is the achievement of the not-yet-achieved, *aprāptasya prāpti*; the second, not uncommon but less well recognized, is the achievement of that which is already achieved, *prāptasya prāpti*.

What is not yet acheived is achieved in time and space by effort. The house you do not have, the spouse, the children, the money, the fame, the health — all that you do not have, require appropriate effort over a period of time to achieve. A place different from the one you occupy is achieved by effort. You walk, run, drive, or fly to it. A clay pot is produced by appropriate effort spent for a period of time on a lump of clay which has only potential form.

These are the achievements we know, achievement, through efforts, of things away from us in time and space. Being dependent upon efforts, these achievements are limited by these very efforts. A given effort, being what it is, is limited in nature. It begins and ends. It is so much and no more. Efforts being limited, the results of efforts also are limited. The product of effort cannot but be limited. The bringing about of a new condition through effort at the same time causes a change in the old condition.

For example:

> Desired achievement: to move from place one to place two.
> Effort: a brisk five minute walk;
> Result: Place two achieved; *place one lost.*

Place one and place two are mutually limiting. The gain of one is the loss of the other. A new condition results in the change of the old condition. The first and the second — the new and the old — are mutually limiting.

It is evident that a result dependent on effort is always limited in nature because effort is limited. So achievements which are not-yet-achieved, *aprāptasya prāpti,* being dependent upon effort, will necessarily be limited. Therefore, the achievement of adequacy, which is the fourth human goal, liberation or *mokṣa,* cannot fall under the heading of the not-yet-achieved, *aprāptasya prāpti.* The adequacy one seeks is nothing less than limitlessness. One seeks to discover oneself as a full, complete, adequate being without even any hint of limitation. This discovery does not — cannot — take place through a process of becoming.

A limited being through limited action gains a limited result. A series of limited results do not add up to limitlessness. A limited being plus a limited result, plus limited results, endlessly, still equals a limited being. By a process of becoming, the inadequate, and limited being will never become limitless. Any changes one brings about, within or without, will not change the limited to the limitless.

All that one does not have — that is removed from one in time and space (including heaven!)—will fall under the heading: not-yet-achieved, *aprāptasya prāpti.* And anything that is separated from one in time or space is limited — wanting. That which is limited and wanting, will remain limited and wanting.

One is not going to be freed from inadequacy at a given place and at a given time or be freed somewhere else, later. This cannot happen. Change of situation, change of place, passage of time are relevant only to something which is limited.

The Gain of the Already-Achieved

The second category of achievement is that of the already-achieved, *prāptasya prāpti.* If adequacy is not the result of the not-yet-achieved, *aprāptasya prāpti,* perhaps it can be an accomplishment of the already-achieved, *prāptasya prāpti.* Is there such a thing as accomplishment of the already-achieved? It seems ridiculous. How can one seek to achieve what is already achieved?

Let us see: A man ardently prays to the Lord to be given a head upon his shoulders.

The Lord appears and says, " No, no. That I cannot give you".

"What", says the devotee, "you call yourself the Almighty Lord but say you cannot do this simple thing which I humbly request?"

"I may be the Lord, but how can I give you, another head at the same location, where you already have one? I can give you a second head, or another head in exchange, or modify the head you have — all of which seem like things which would be useful to you — but I cannot give you a head where you already have a head."

There can be no achievement of the already-achieved such as obtaining a head where a head already is. The existing object (a head) stands in the way of the gain of a second object (another head) in an identical time-space locus.

However, there is another kind of situation where achievement of the already-achieved appears to be possible. When you have something but do not realize that you have it, ignorance of what is possessed can cause you to seek what is already in fact in your possession. You can have something and not realize that you have it. Non-recognition of something can cause one to seek the very thing that is in one's possession.

Achievement of the already-achieved becomes possible when ignorance prevents one from knowing the fact that the thing is already there.

For example: Resting a moment from my studies, I automatically push my reading glasses up from my eyes until the lenses rest on the top of my head. Returning to my book a few minutes later, I search the desk and the table, the chest of the drawers, and the floor, for my missing glasses, unaware that they are with me, precariously perched on my own head.

"Someone has taken my glasses", I cry; "I must have them; I need them; I must find them". All the time my glasses are with me. Only ignorance of that fact keeps me away from them.

When I am searching for glasses which are on the top of my head, there is no distance in space or time between me, the seeker, *sādhaka,* of the glasses and me, the possessor of the glasses, the end to be achieved, the *sādhya.* With the glasses forgotten, perched on my head, I want to be the possessor of my glasses. I am a seeker, *sādhaka,* of the state of being the possessor of my glasses. Because the glasses are on the top of my head, I am the goal, *sādhya,* the possessor of my glasses.

The distance between me, the seeker of the glasses, and me, the sought, the possessor of the glasses, is ignorance alone. Thus, in the situation where one is ignorant of the fact that what one seeks is already there, there is such a thing as the achievement of the already-achieved; in such a situation one's ignorance creates an apparent distance.

Freedom from Inadequacy: an Already-Achieved Goal

The first three human goals, *dharma, artha, kāma,* the ethical pursuit of security and pleasures, deal with not-yet-acheived gains; gains which, distant from the seeker in time and space, must be gained by effort. Effort being inherently limited, produces a limited result.

The fourth human goal, freedom from inadequacy, limitlessness, *mokṣa,* is not, *cannot* be, produced by limited effort. Freedom from inadequacy, *mokṣa,* cannot be a not-yet-achieved goal to be gained through effort. Perhaps, then, *mokṣa* may be an already-achieved goal hidden from the seeker by the ignorance of the seeker. Inquiry into the nature of adequacy shows that this is the only category in which we can put *mokṣa.*

If freedom from inadequacy, *mokṣa,* is already achieved, this means that like the possessor of the glasses who wants to find the glasses, I *am* the adequate self who yet wants to become the adequate self. I am the adequate self and yet I seek the adequate self; this can only mean that somehow ignorance hides me, the sought, from me, the seeker.

The Informed Seeker

It has been said that the seeker of adequacy, *mokṣa,* is called a *mumukṣu.* Such a seeker has discovered that the basic human problem underlying all pursuits is the urge to be completely free from inadequacy and has realized that the pursuit of security and pleasures cannot bring this freedom. When the direct seeker of freedom further discovers that the goal he seeks must fall under the head of the already-achieved, another dimension is added to his understanding. He is then in a position to understand what means are available to him to gain his goal.

When I, a seeker directly pursuing freedom from all inadequacy, discover that what I seek is not something apart from me, something yet to-be-achieved, but is something separated from me only by ignorance, my goal becomes the destruction of that ignorance: then I seek knowledge.

When you know that you are not different from what you seek, then you become an informed *mumukṣu*. You know you are seeking knowledge. An informed *mumukṣu* is called a *jijñāsu:*

mumukṣu	One who desires freedom from inadequacy;
jijñāsu	One who desires knowledge for the sake of freedom from inadequacy.

A *mumukṣu* who has not discovered that knowledge is what is required may do many, futile things in his search for liberation. A seeker observant enough to see that his usual pursuits do not produce adequacy but who has not understood that adequacy cannot be produced by any kind of effort, may resort to harsh austerities, hoping to win the freedom he has not been able to achieve by usual efforts. Many examples can be found in almost all religions of severe, painful, and sometimes strange practices undertaken for the sake of deliverance from limitation.

Every *mumukṣu*, every *seeker*, will become a *jijñāsu* (one who seeks not to *do* something but to *know* something) when he understands the nature of the problem. The problem is to dispel self-ignorance. The solution is to gain self-knowledge.

The adequate being that I want to be can never be attained through a process of becoming. The fact must be that I am already an adequate being, even though I seek to be an adequate being. The separation between me and adequacy must be due to ignorance. Therefore, it is ignorance, self-ignorance that must go. For self-ignorance to go, there must be self-knowledge. Self-knowledge is what is called liberation.

For self-knowledge, self-inquiry is necessary. Inquiry is necessary because of the contradictory information my experiences have given me about myself. I have had two types of experiences: one type of experience has led me to conclude that I am inadequate; another type has shown me to be an adequate being. I need to reconcile these two types of experiences to see the fact that I am an adequate being. To accomplish this reconciliation I must conduct a self-inquiry called *ātma-vicāra*. This inquiry into the self which leads to discovery of the nature of oneself, is called Vedānta.

CHAPTER FOUR

Ignorance and Knowledge

There are two types of achievements: achievement of something not-yet-achieved, and achievement of what is already-achieved. Freedom from inadequacy, *mokṣa,* cannot be of the first kind because achievement of the not-yet-achieved involves change produced by effort. Change is always limited. The previous condition and the succeeding condition mutually limit each other. All gain through change involves loss. There is never any absolute gain. Completeness—total adequacy—cannot be an achievement of the not-yet-achieved. If such an achievement is possible, it must be of the second kind: an achievement of the already-achieved. Everyday experiences reveal examples of such achievements. A situation in which someone is searching for his reading glasses, unaware that the glasses are perched on the top of his head, is an example of an already-achieved goal. The one who seeks to be the possessor of the glasses is already the possessor of the glasses. The seeker is not different from the sought. The apparent difference between the seeker and the sought is brought about by ignorance.

Everyone is Born Ignorant

Just as one can be ignorant of one's glasses sitting atop one's head, one can be ignorant of oneself. In fact there is no reason why one should know oneself. Everyone is born vastly ignorant. Not absolutely ignorant, because even a tiny infant knows a few, basic things: to ask for food; to fear a fall; to recognize a smile although his ignorance is immense.

The vast ignorance of the newborn includes the ignorance of the self. The ignorance with which one begins life includes ignorance of oneself as well as ignorance of everything else. As one is ignorant of other things, like mother, father, language, arithmetic, so, too, one is ignorant of oneself. Every form of ignorance is present—self-ignorance included.

The Shedding of Ignorance

Ignorance is shed as one gains valid knowledge. Valid knowledge requires an appropriate *pramāṇa*, an appropriate instrument, or means of knowledge.

pramā-karaṇam	*pramāṇa m*
knowledge-instrument	means of knowledge

Certain means of knowledge—the five sense organs supported by an attentive mind—are given to us for knowing the world. It is very natural to make use of these means at our disposal. If one's eyes and ears are open, and the mind simultaneously alert, one sees and hears. Similarly, one smells, tastes, experiences the sense of touch. In a newborn child, the sense organs are not fully functional. Function develops gradually. As the child develops, the capacity of the sense organs increases. Later, as the adult ages, the capacity declines. It is through these means of knowledge, the senses supported by the mind, that one sheds one's ignorance of the world and gains knowledge—a working knowledge of the world. Thus, as one gains knowledge, one sheds ignorance. Ignorance is not gained. Ignorance is one thing for which one need not work. Everyone is born with ignorance in abundance.

As one grows, through the use of valid means of knowledge, one sheds ignorance, *ajñāna*. When the senses and the mind are not defective, perception, the use of the senses supported by the mind, gives rise to a valid working knowledge. Perceptual knowledge is the "working knowledge" of the world, valid in its own sphere.

The family encourages this process of learning and at the same time makes language available as part of the knowledge to be gained. The mother says, "this is an apple", "this is a chair", "this is a table", "this is a flower". The father adds, "this is your hand", "this is a stone", "these are two stones". As a child one looks, touches, tastes, smells, and listens to the sound that is a word naming the object perceived. In this way, ignorance is shed and knowledge gained, first of forms and names, then of colour and other attributes; then later come finer distinctions, shades of colour, various sizes and shapes. Thus forms and names and finer and yet finer distinctions are acquired. And knowledge is gained of actions too—of walking, talking, eating; and of categories, classes of things, and the connections between and among them.

Connections : *sambandha*

As one acquires more and more perceptual knowledge, one is able to perceive certain connections between different things; between classes of things; between different actions; between actions and things. These special relationships or connections are called *sambandha.* From these relationships we are able to make certain inferences. Such inferences are called *vyāpti-jñāna.*

vyāpti	invariable concomitance
jñāna	knowledge
I see smoke.	I infer fire.

I have *vyāpti jñāna,* inferential knowledge of fire.

Thus, the knowledge of certain relationships allows me to make certain inferences from my perceptions. Inferential knowledge is perception-based.

Through perception and perception-born inference one gathers knowledge of the world. And the validity of perceptual and perception-based knowledge is established by its practicability in the world.

Objects are Known through Perception

The perceptual means of knowledge, the five sense organs, are the valid means for knowing things which the sense organs can objectify. Each sense organ has an appropriate object for objectification: the eyes, form and colour; the ears, sound; the nose, smell; the tongue, taste; the body, touch. My five sense organs objectify the five appropriate sense objects external to them and with these senses, supported by my mind, I gain knowledge of all the things I can objectify.

The Means of Knowledge Must be Appropriate

In the light of the knowledge gained through one's senses, the ignorance of the world goes away. Ignorance never goes away unless knowledge, its opposite, is born. The birth of knowledge always requires a valid means of knowledge. The means must be appropriate to the particular knowledge sought. What can be gained through one means of knowledge cannot be gained by another means. If you want to know the colour of the flower in your hand, the ear won't do; nor can the eye tell you if it is fragrant. The sense organs, each one of them, is capable of acquiring a given form of knowledge—objectifying a particular object in a given way. The valid, appropriate means for knowledge is determined by the nature of the particular knowledge sought.

If the particular knowledge sought is the colour of some object, open your eyes and look. If the object is too far away for your short-sighted eyes to determine its shade, it will do you no good to try to "hear" its colour with your keen ears. Get stronger eye glasses; borrow some binoculars; but you have to use your eyes. Ears, no matter how sharp, cannot do the job. The particular knowledge of a particular object requires appropriate means for that knowledge.

Inferences are Perception-based

Inferences, too are basically perception because they are dependent upon data from the senses. All inferences are based on perceptual data. Technological progress has brought about enhancement of the sensory capability. Our capacity to perceive has been greatly improved by various instruments which have been developed: microscopes, telescopes, x-ray machines, radar devices, and so forth. With improved sensory data, our knowledge has grown.

All increase of knowledge as a result of enhanced perception, bringing increased opportunity for inference, still remains no more than knowledge about things which can be objectified.

With improved sensory data, knowledge keeps improving. This improved knowledge is always about something which can be objectified. Whether the knowledge is about a cell, or an atom, or the universe itself, it is about something subject to objectification. Even psychology is knowledge about something that can be objectified. One's thoughts, responses, and attitudes can be observed—objectified—and from that objectification some generalizations can be made. Thus, a new discipline of knowledge is born.

The knowledge acquisition we have been discussing so far is of things, objects. Perception is always of an object. Inference is based upon perception. Therefore, all inferences (and presumptions), being what they are, are about objects alone. [1]

---

1. The word "object" is being used in its grammatical sense of something other than the subject, oneself, not in the general sense of something tangible. This usage of object can be understood through grammatical analysis of sentence structure.

I	know	an atom.
subject	*predicate*	*object*

Object means anything the subject objectifies. Any given thing the subject comes to know, he objectifies.

Intellectual Knowledge is Inferential Knowledge

What one calls "intellectual knowledge" is nothing but inferential knowledge. Such intellectual knowledge, too, has its basis in the perception of objects. There is no intellectual knowledge which is not, finally, based on objects. Intellectual is inferential and all perceptual and inferential knowledge is of objects—of things other than oneself.

Knowledge is not Created

The gaining of knowledge is nothing but the shedding of ignorance. The moment I come to know what a pot is like, my ignorance of pot is gone. Similarly, when I come to know what a cell is like, then my ignorance of cell, to the extent that I know about the cell, is removed.

Ignorance is something one is born with. Knowledge is nothing but the shedding of it, *ajñāna nivṛtti*. The gain of knowledge is not a creation, *sṛṣṭi*. The gain of knowledge is only a negation—negation of ignorance. Knowledge is covered with ignorance. All one does is remove ignorance; then knowledge is so to speak gained. Knowledge is not something produced or created. Knowledge always is. Knowledge is what is.

By removing ignorance one uncovers knowledge.

ajñāna-nivṛtti = *jñāna*
ignorance, causing the removal of = knowledge

Valid Knowledge

Knowledge is valid when it is true to what is. When it is true to what is, it cannot later be negated. When the word *jñāna,* knowledge, is used, it should be used to mean completely valid knowledge; knowledge that is *abādhitam,* not subject to later negation.

For the most part, the knowledge one gathers is not completely valid but is a "working knowledge" of the world. Working knowledge is a relatively valid knowledge, which can be negated; but is none the less useful. That the sun will rise in the east tomorrow morning at a certain time is working knowledge based on sensory data. This knowledge can be negated. it is relatively valid only from a given standpoint. More complete understanding of the fact reveals that the sun does not rise. But the working knowledge of sunrise at a particular place and time is useful knowledge, helpful in planning one's activities.

Through the five senses backed by the mind one goes on gaining knowledge and shedding ignorance about things other than oneself. The knowledge gained is about things that can be objectified, not about oneself, the non-objectifiable subject. Objects are things other than oneself, the subject. I possess valid instruments to gain a working knowledge of objects. Sensory perception and sense-based inference are the valid means of my knowledge of all the things I can objectify. This is what perception, including all forms of enhanced perception, is perception, is meant for—to know things that can be objectified. Inference, too, perception-based as it is, is a means of knowing things other than myself.

Perception is Useless for Knowing Oneself

I am the subject. I am the knower. Do I have a valid means of knowledge for knowing myself? Perception and inference do not reveal the subject. Perception and perception-based inference are useless for knowing the subject—they work only for things which the sense organs can objectify. One can use perception well and come to enjoy a high level of information about objects and still be ignorant about oneself. One can be a very well-informed person, learned in various disciplines of knowledge with many achievements to one's credit, and still continue to be ignorant of oneself. Self-knowledge is not necessary to operate the means of knowledge—the senses backed by the mind—for knowing objects. One need not have self-knowledge to be proficient in any of the usual disciplines of knowledge.

So far as we know, non-human creatures do not have sufficiently self-conscious evolved minds to inquire into the nature of themselves. None the less, they successfully use perception and inference. Some kind of perception and some use of inference seem available to all beings. The migratory behaviour of birds indicates an ability to make inferences; their navigation requires inference. Bats are able to determine the location and type of objects by reading echoes; they conduct their affairs on the inferences drawn from these data.

A cow presumably has neither self-consciousness nor self-knowledge, but its ignorance is not a problem. A cow does not say to itself, "I know I am the finest breed of cow who gives many litres of milk each day, but I do not seem to be satisfied with this role. I wonder what my real nature is. Surely, I must be something more than a living milk machine". A cow is not bothered by self-knowledge or self-ignorance. Its only problems are those of hunger, thirst, warmth and survival. Unconcerned with self-ignorance, lacking self-consciousness, the cow none the less conducts its affairs through perception and, at least, rudimentary inference.

In the *Brahmasutra Bhāṣya* there is a classic description of the cow's ability to infer: A man and a cow are standing in a meadow. The man pulls out a bunch of grass and calls out to the cow. She turns her head and looks at him. He smiles, extending his arm and beckoning to her with the hand holding the grass. She looks and thinks. Eating grass is *iṣṭa-sādhana,* a desirable objective, especially eating grass obtained with no effort. She remembers, that this happened a few times in the past. "People like this one have fed me good grass. It was nice." "Come", calls the man. The cow looks at him closely. He appears benevolent. The cow makes up her mind, "I am being offered a harmless, pleasant experience". She has made an inferential conclusion based on her present perceptions and remembered past perceptions; she begins to amble slowly towards the man.

After a few seconds the man drops the bunch of grass, bends over and picks up a large stick. The cow stops in her tracks and looks closely. The man raises the stick over his head and scowls angrily. The cow quickly reaches a new inferential conlusion. "This fellow may be about to beat me with that stick—a very unpleasant experience." She tosses her head, turns, and trots quickly away.

Both decisions, to first approach the man and then to run away from him are the result of perception-based inference. Thus the cow, in spite of its self-ignorance, is quite able to make inferential conclusions.

Human beings are more skilled in gathering perceptual data and making inferences than a cow or, so far as we know, any other animal. We enhance our perceptions with powerful instruments, adding to the capacity of our sense organs. We have developed keen disciplines of logic which enable us to make better inferences from the data we gather. But no matter what data are gathered or inferences drawn, leading to proficiency in countless branches of knowledge about things, the human being can remain as self-ignorant as the cow. For, knowledge gathered about objects does not destroy self-ignorance.

The Need for Knowledge of Oneself

If there is a solution to the peculiar human problem of one's constant struggle for completeness, then that solution lies in knowledge alone. When it has become clear to me that it is not possible for me to become a complete, adequate being through the gain or loss of things, nor can I rid myself of the urge to become an adequate being, then I know I *must* gain knowledge of myself. The adequate being I want to be cannot be produced by a process of becoming. No action can produce limitlessness; therefore, there is only one way out—not the one of action, but the one of knowledge.

If my problem has a solution, it can only be through the knowledge of myself. To gain the limitlessness I seek, I must already be that fully adequate being whose adequacy is hidden by ignorance. I need a means to shed that ignorance.

The Means to Gain Knowledge of Oneself

Where can one find means to discover the nature of oneself, the subject, I? As a knower, the subject revealed by the first person singular I, I am ignorant of myself. I am the subject, the knower, behind the mind and the sense organs but from childhood onwards I, the subject, am unknown to myself. In the beginning I was ignorant of myself and most other things. As I grow, I gain knowledge of many things through perception and inference. But my ignorance of myself remains. I want to shed that self-ignorance. Is there an appropriate, valid means of knowledge of myself? Perception and inference are useful only for things which can be objectified. I, the subject, cannot be objectified. Perception and perception-based inferences are all relevant only for knowledge of objects other than "I". By definition, sense data and inference are means of knowledge for things which the subject can objectify. If the subject is objectified, it no longer is the subject but only another object—and that which objectifies it is the sought-for subject. How can I gain knowledge of myself, I, the ultimate, non-objectifiable subject?

The *Muṇḍaka Upaniṣad* verse we came across describes the need for knowledge and also tells what to do to gain that knowledge:

> *parīkṣya lokān karmacitān brāhmaṇo*
> *nirvedamāyānnāstyakṛtaḥ kṛtena*
> *tadvijñānārthaṁ sa gurumevābhigacchet*
> *samitpāṇiḥ śrotriyaṁ brahmaniṣṭham*
>
> (I,ii, 12 *Muṇḍaka Upaniṣad*)

Having analysed the worldly experiences achieved through effort, a mature person gains dispassion, discerns that the uncreated (limitlessness) cannot be produced by action.

To know That (the uncreated limitlessness), he, with twigs in hand, should go to a teacher who is learned in the scriptures, and steadfast in the knowledge of himself.

The mature person recognizes from examination of his own worldly experiences that what he seeks is adequacy, and is able to see that the things for which he has been struggling cannot bring that adequacy. He gains a dispassion towards security, *artha,* and pleasures, *kāma.* Basically, he seeks nothing less than limitlessness itself. The gain of the limited cannot produce limitlessness. Limitlessness by nature is uncreated, *akṛta.* By action, *kṛtena,* the uncreated is not produced.

To know that uncreated limitlessness which cannot be produced, which can only be known, but not by such means as perception and inference, one has to go to a teacher, a *guru,* "with twigs in hand"—which means with hands ready to serve, and with the right attitude. This verse tells what a *mumukṣu,* an informed seeker of freedom from limitation should do. An informed seeker knows that his search is for knowledge; he has become a *jijñāsu,* one who desires knowledge. For that knowledge he must go to a teacher, a *guru.*

For Knowledge of Oneself, Go to a Qualified Guru

A *guru* is one who dispels darkness. The word itself reveals the function; *gu* stands for darkness; *ru* means the one who dispels darkness. A *guru* then, is a dispeller of darkness. He doesn't produce anything. He doesn't even produce knowledge. He throws light on something that is already there. A *guru* is a teacher, who has the capacity to dispel the ignorance covering whatever it is one wants to know. If I want to end my ignorance of astronomy, I need to find someone who knows something about the stars and the planets. It will not do me any good to go to a marine biologist who cannot distinguish a galaxy from a constellation. I must find someone who has lost his ignorance in the area of my interest; someone who has the knowledge I seek.

A teacher does not produce anything; he does not need to produce anything. Nobody can produce knowledge. Knowledge is the accurate appreciation of what is. The teacher throws light upon something which is already there. If an object I want to see is in a completely dark room, all I need is light to see it in. The light does not produce the object; it merely dispels the darkness so that I can see it. A light in a dark room produces neither the room nor the objects in it; it only reveals what *is*.

Similarly, to dispel my ignorance of myself, what is needed is light. Am I the inadequate, limited being I generally see myself to be? Or, am I the complete, whole being I long to be—my completeness somehow hidden from me by ignorance? To answer this question, a teacher is needed—a teacher with appropriate knowledge to throw light upon my nature. If the teacher has knowledge of *his* own nature, is that appropriate knowledge to illumine *my* nature? A *guru* with self-knowledge can throw light upon his self; but does that light give him knowledge of *my* self, too? If my self and his self are the same, he will know my self if he knows his own. He will be able to throw light on my self for me from his knowledge of his own self. However, if the *guru's* self is peculiar, differing from mine then, perhaps, his knowledge will be of no use to me.

The possible peculiarity of the *guru's* self is not a problem because the adequate self which one seeks, the adequate self which the *guru* knows, cannot have any peculiarity and yet be the adequate self. Adequacy has no peculiarity. Adequacy is totality, completeness; adequacy is without any limitation; adequacy is limitlessness which can suffer no duality. Adequacy can only be one; oneness without a second. There cannot be two limitlessnesses. When there are two, each limits the other.

Therefore, the verse says *tam gurum abhigacchet,* go to *that guru; that guru* who can throw light upon the uncreated, the limitless self. *Guru* means teacher, not just teacher of a particular subject. *Guru* means any teacher who by means of communication can throw light on a subject that he knows and which the student wishes to know. To be a valid *guru* worthy of the label, one must be able to throw light on ignorance.

The student, because he wants to know, is willing to serve the teacher. The student is a *jijñāsu,* one characterized by wanting to know. A *jijñāsu* wants to know—whatever the cost—so he goes to the teacher with a readiness to serve, with a fresh open mind, with a loving heart. The verse indicates this attitude by saying *samitpaniḥ,* "with twigs in hand", bringing fuel for the teacher's fire, a traditional way of showing willingness to serve the teacher.

And what does the teacher do? He teaches. That is all he has to do. What is teaching? Teaching, for the most part, is nothing but words. What do words do? Words are a means of knowledge. No doubt, like inference, they are dependent upon perception, but at the same time, they also can be an independent means of knowledge. Sometimes words do what one's sense organs cannot do. Words depend upon perception—the hearing of the ears or the seeing of the eyes; but ears only hear sounds; eyes only see forms. It is the informed mind that turns sound and form into words. When the mind undergoes the discipline of language, the sounds heard are no longer meaningless sounds but become meaningful sounds; the forms seen become meaningful forms. Words, thus, have an independence from their simple perception as sound which allows them to give rise to knowledge that the simple perception does not reveal. Words encode past perceptions; words make possible the analysis of the connections between perceptions in the absence of the perceived objects. Words can become an independent means of knowledge which can reveal both known and unknown things to one.

Consider for example that a friend has returned from a visit to some exotic place and he describes to me a very unusual bird. A bird with an emerald beak, ruby feet, gold and silver wings. I know what a bird is, what the parts of a bird are, and the colour and appearance of precious stones and metals; therefore, from his words I am able to gain knowledge of a thing unknown to me, a strange bird which I have never seen.

This knowledge is gained through words, *śabda,* which constitute an independent means of knowledge.

Indirect and Direct Knowledge from Words

Words can give indirect or direct knowledge, depending on the relationship between the knower and the object. If the object is away from the knower's immediate experience, words can only give rise to indirect knowledge; if the object is within the range of the knower's immediate experience, words can bring about direct knowledge. The bird with the emerald beak, described above, was known only by indirect knowledge. Not having seen the bird myself, my knowledge of the bird rests upon the words of my friend. The weight I give to that knowledge depends upon my faith in the accuracy of his perception and his truthfulness. Similarly, I can gain indirect knowledge of many things not directly known to me. Indirect knowledge becomes direct knowledge when confirmed by experience.

For example: Someone gives a detailed description of the appearance and flavour of the tropical jackfruit to a person who has never seen or tasted jackfruit.

Subsequently, the latter comes to India where he has the opportunity to sample many tropical fruits strange to him. One day while eating an unknown fruit he tells his host, "This is very good, but some day I would like very much to try jackfruit; I have heard so much about it". Words have given him indirect knowledge of this fruit. His host replies, "It is jackfruit you are now eating", imparting knowledge of something the guest is at the time experiencing. "Oh", says the traveller, "now I know jackfruit".

Words have brought him direct knowledge.

The Words of the Guru give Direct Knowledge of the Self

What kind of knowledge can the words of a teacher give about oneself? Indirect or direct? I seek knowledge of myself, of "I". Where is this I? Is it near me or away from me? It is neither. It is I, immediate. Words throwing light on oneself will give direct knowledge of "I". Either they must give direct knowledge or no knowledge at all.

When the teacher, the *guru,* who has knowledge of himself teaches, he will throw light on the me which is here, now, the available, immediate me; the knowledge will be direct, immediate knowledge.

That is why the teacher of self-knowledge and the teaching are regarded as sacred; they are a direct means of knowledge of oneself. The teaching is a body of knowledge in the form of words and sentences—known as Vedanta—which throws light upon oneself. Vedanta is called a *śabda pramāṇa,* a verbal means of knowledge. Through words, it is a direct means of knowledge of oneself.

CHAPTER FIVE
The Teacher

The Gain of Adequacy Requires Knowledge, not Action

To gain anything which is away from one in time or space requires a change. Change involves effort, the exerted force called action, *karma.* Every change involves a loss. Gain through change involves the loss of the prior condition. The limitless, adequate being that one wants to be, cannot be the product of a process of change. One cannot *become* totally adequate, complete, because the new condition gained excludes the relinquished old condition. A "becoming", being what it is, is always limited in nature. There is no absolute gain in any becoming. To be a fully adequate being is to have an absolute gain. An absolute gain is not possible in the relative world. So, the adequate being can never be the end product of a process of becoming.

Therefore, the gain of the adequacy that everyone seeks, has to be a gain that does not involve a process of becoming; it has to be a gain without effort. The only thing that can be gained without effort is something that has been gained already; something that is already there. It is necessary to "gain" something that is already there when that something is separated from the seeker, not by time or distance, but by ignorance. If the seeker does not know that what he seeks is there, it will be "as though" away from him. To gain such a thing requires not action, but knowledge. Knowledge depends upon the operation of a valid means of knowledge. We have means of knowledge for objects other than ourselves. The senses provide the data for knowing objects. All objects other than oneself can be known from perceptual data and perception-based inference. But what is the means of knowing the knower, the subject? There does not seem to be a way at one's disposal to know oneself, the knower, who knows the objects. The subject cannot be known through the objectification of perception and inference. A "subject", when objectifed, becomes an object. It is not possible to objectify oneself and still look at oneself. If I become the object, I am no longer the subject. The subject-I cannot be the object-I. Whatever is objectified can no longer be considered the subject who is looking and, it is that "looker-subject" that I seek to know. Is it a hopeless dilemma? Am I stuck with self-ignorance?

Words, a Valid Means of Knowledge

For knowing oneself there is a need for a valid means of knowledge capable of dispelling self-ignorance — some means other than sense-based perception and inference. It has been seen that words, *śabda,* in their own right, independent of perception, can be a valid means of knowledge. Words are based on sounds heard (or forms seen), but it is not the sense data that are the word; the sense data only carry the word to an informed mind — a mind that recognizes certain sounds or forms as language. It is the sound or form as word, that brings knowledge. The knowledge brought by words can be direct or indirect. Whether the words bring direct or indirect knowledge depends upon the object. If the object is beyond the scope of one's perception or experience, the knowledge born will be indirect. Indirect knowledge, no matter how useful, is never completely true to the object. It is always subject to a later modification upon direct knowledge. However, if the object is not away from one but is at hand, experienced but not recognized, then words can give direct knowledge, a knowledge true to the nature of the object. For example, there is a well-known story that shows how words can give knowledge, both direct and indirect.

The Story of the Tenth Man

Ten students were given permission by their *guru* to go on a pilgrimage. In the course of their journey, they crossed a swift river. After the crossing, the leader of the group, responsible for their safety, assembled them on the river bank and counted them. He counted nine. The tenth student was missing. He counted again, very slowly, up to nine. Still there was one missing. The leader looked all around, but nowhere could the tenth man be seen. He counted again: nine only. He stood there in shock and despair thinking of the sad message he would have to take back to their teacher: "One man has been lost".

An old man standing a short distance away, had been watching this scene. He walked over to the sorrowful leader and asked, "Why are you so upset?" The leader, pointing to his companions, answered, "When we started on our pilgrimage this morning there were ten of us; now that we have crossed this river, there are only nine". The old man looked at the group and asked, "You say there were ten of you when you started out?" "Yes". "Now you say there are only nine?" "Yes. The tenth one cannot be found. He must have drowned", replied the trembling leader. The old man smiled a little and said "Don't worry. The tenth man got across the river with you. He is here now. I'II show him to you".

The old man seemed wise and sincere; relief swept over the young leader. "Did you hear that?" he called out to the group gathered around. "The tenth man *is!*" One of the students was more sceptical. "How can you say that?" he asked the leader; "Have you seen the tenth man?" "No", said the leader, "I have not yet seen the tenth man, but this gentleman says he exists and I believe him".

At this juncture in the story, the leader has only indirect knowledge that the tenth man exists. Through the words of the old man he has gained indirect knowledge, called *parokṣa jñānam,* of the existence of the tenth man. Previously he had come to the conclusion that the tenth man probably had drowned and had been swept away by the river; but now his faith in the truth of the old man's words lets him accept, even without personal verification, that the tenth man exists. The leader's mind is no longer closed and agitated. It is in a more neutral frame with some faith in a happy outcome. The neutral frame of mind is a receptive mind, ready for knowledge — able to accept that the fact can be discovered, knowledge can be gained. The leader has faith in the correctness of the indirect knowledge, a faith that the indirect knowledge will be confirmed by direct knowledge. It is faith, *śraddhā,* pending discovery — an openness and positive expectation. The leader has no reason to disbelieve the words of the old man, and his credibility is given weight by the fact that the old man has said "I will show the tenth man to you *here, now*", not sometime later in some other place. The old man has said that he will at the present time, in the present place produce the tenth man. He has not told the leader that there is anything the leader must do in order that the tenth man can be produced — to bring about the tenth man. The promise held out by the old man does not involve effort on the part of the leader or change of place or passage of time.

The story continues: The old man tells the leader, "Please bring all the other boys here in front of me and have them arrange themselves in a line". The leader, his eyes still red from weeping over the loss of his fellow student, quickly responds. "Now", says the old man, "come stand by my side and count these fellows one more time". The leader's heart sinks; he is reluctant to go through one more sad, useless count. None the less, he has faith in the old man, and reluctant though he feels, but because the old man has requested it, he counts one more time up to nine, and turns to the old man, "Sir! Where *is* the tenth man?" he demands.

The old man says: "*tat tvam asi*, That thou art. You are the tenth man. You, the leader who forgot to count himself, are the tenth man you are seeking."

The Problem when the Seeker is the Sought

Any seeking is a denial of the presence of the sought. The act of seeking denies that the sought is in the presence of the seeker. The presence of the seeking denies the presence of the sought. In the story of the tenth man, the seeker is the sought. When the seeker is the sought, the presence of the sought is denied at the very place where it is to be found. A search in which the seeker and the sought are identical is inherently likely to fail. The very status of being a seeker means that you have concluded that what you seek is not in your presence; this conclusion ensures that you will not look where what you want is to be found. The presence of you as a seeker denies you as the sought. The best place to hide something is where it is thought not to be. If it is hidden at a place where it is denied, or thought not to be, it is, indeed, well hidden.

So the moment the tenth man started seeking, the place where the sought was to be found was denied. But the tenth man, seeing his group as incomplete, had no choice but to search for the missing man who would complete the number, a search which excluded the sought. The nature of this kind of situation must be very clearly seen — and grasped fully.

When the seeker and the sought are identical, any small attempt on the part of the seeker to gain the sought will deny the presence of the sought at the place where it is to be found.

In such a situation, for the seeker to "gain" what he seeks, he must be relieved of seeing himself as a seeker; he must be freed, for the time being, from the need to gain the sought. The old man, by promising to reveal the missing tenth man, freed the leader's mind from the status of a seeker. That mind, even though it had not discovered the presence of the tenth man, became imbued with a faith, *śraddhā,* that the discovery would be made, allowing it to abide in a certain freshness and receptivity. From a sentence, then, the free, fresh, receptive mind was able to discover, I am what I seek; I am the tenth man".

Teaching through Words in a Context

The statement of the old man, "That thou art", was a teaching, *upadeśa,* which imparted knowledge to the student. The knowledge was imparted by words spoken by the teacher in a context the teacher had created.

The context — the interrelated conditions surrounding the words — is an important factor in the ability of words to convey the meaning intended by the teacher.

The old man did not just make a bald declaration, uncaring of whether it would be believed. Instead he assembled all the students and allowed the leader to commit his mistake again so that he may discover what had happened. The leader was led to see for himself, through words spoken in a specially created context, that he had left himself out — that he was the missing man he sought.

General Knowledge and Particular Knowledge

From the old man, the sorrowful student leader obtained *viśeṣa jñānam*, a peculiar, different, extra knowledge which enhanced his general knowledge, *sāmānya jñānam*, of the situation. Prior to hearing the words of the old man the student leader did not know that he, himself, was the tenth man. He did not have that particular knowledge, *viśeṣajñānam,* of the tenth man and of himself but he certainly was not without some knowledge of both the tenth man and himself. It took some knowledge of the tenth man for him to become a seeker of the tenth man. If he had no knowledge whatsoever of the existence of a tenth man, he would have had no basis for missing him, no basis for committing a mistake about his identity. But he did have some knowledge. He knew that the person who seemed to be missing was a man and a student and that he had been present at the *āśrama* when their *guru* had counted out their number before sending them on the trip. Even without any help from the old man, the leader had a great store of knowledge about himself. He could describe himself physically; he could name his relatives; he could identify his location, his possessions. He knew that he was a student on a pilgrimage, that he was the leader of the group, that he was standing on the bank of a river. So he had knowledge of himself. But he didn't have the particular knowledge that *he* was the tenth man. It was the lack of that particular knowledge that the tenth man was himself which made him a seeker of the tenth man. When he gained that particular knowledge from the old man he ceased to be a seeker.

Self-Ignorance is not Total Ignorance of Self

When it is said that one is self-ignorant, this does not mean that one is totally without knowledge of oneself. If one were totally ignorant about oneself, a mistake about oneself could not be committed. If I did not have the kind of evolved mind that can appreciate "I am", then I would not consider myself to be an inadequate being. If "I am" is unknown to me then I cannot conclude that "I am inadequate". When I have no consciousness of an object, I do not commit a mistake with regard to it. However, when I am conscious of something but don't recognize it for what it is, it is then that I commit a mistake.

"I am" is very much known to me. I know that I am here now. I know "I am" exists. The question is, "Do I correctly recognize that existing 'I am' for what it is?" If I am the adequate being I long to be but fail to recognize that fact, then I shall conclude that I am inadequate and strive to become adequate — a futile effort. Adequacy cannot be gained through change or through action. Adequacy can only be gained through recognition of it as the existent fact which has been hidden from me by ignorance.

When something is an immediate, existent fact, not recognized out of ignorance, words can produce direct knowledge of that fact. The words "you are the tenth man" spoken in the appropriate context, produced immediate knowledge of the presence of the tenth man for the leader of the students.

If, in fact, adequacy is one's nature, then when a teacher creates the appropriate context for the words to convey their meaning, the statement, *tat tvam asi*, "that thou art" — you are that adequate being you seek to be — can give direct knowledge of oneself as an adequate being.

What the Teacher Must Know

For a teacher to be able to use words to give direct knowledge not only must the object of knowledge be present but the teacher, himself, must both be free from ignorance about the object and know how to create a context in which words can destroy the student's ignorance. For the old man to be able to use words to impart immediate knowledge of the tenth man, he had to have completely and directly shed his ignorance of the identity of the tenth man. If the students had scattered along the bank with some out of sight before the old man had an opportunity to count them all for himself, then he would not have had direct knowledge of the tenth man. He might have had a plausible theory that could be proved later, but he would not have had the kind of knowledge that enabled him to state categorically that he could immediately produce the tenth man. Had the old man missed seeing the tenth man, he would have had only more ignorance to impart.

For words to produce direct, immediate knowledge the teacher must clearly know what he sets out to impart by words and, in the presence of the object of knowledge, the correct context must be established.

The old man had to see clearly that the leader himself was the tenth man. Had he not known that he could not have held out the assurance that he could produce the tenth man. The old man was a good teacher. He recognized the problem and he knew what he was doing in setting the context before revealing who the tenth man was. The teacher must himself know the tenth man to be able to reveal him.

The Teacher should know Adequacy as Himself

To reveal adequacy to the seeker, teacher should know adequacy himself, and he should know how to establish a context in which adequacy is discovered. The *Muṇḍaka* verse we have discussed describes that teacher:

> *gurumeva abhigacchet ...*
> *śrotriyam brahmaniṣṭh a m*
>
> Go to a teacher who is learned in the subject matter, and steadfast in that knowledge.

The teacher whose words can be a direct means of self-knowledge is one who is both *Śrotriyam* and *brahmaniṣṭham*. *Śrotriyam* means one who is well-versed in the scriptural source of the teaching, one who knows the content of the texts and also the methodology for imparting that knowledge. *Śrotriyam* derives from the verbal root which means "to hear" and indicates, in accordance with the oral tradition of teaching, the one who is versed in the knowledge of the adequate being, having heard that knowledge from its proper sources. *Brahmaniṣṭh a m* is one who knows adequacy; who absolutely knows "I am a complete being".

One who is *brahmaniṣṭham* knows *brahman* as himself, not as something other than himself. *Brahman*, derived from a word which means "to grow, to increase", indicates "bigness", or "limitlessness". *Niṣṭha* means "steadfastness". The one who is *brahmaniṣṭham* is one who is steadfast in the knowledge of himself as the full, complete, limitless being.

The teacher who can teach you that you are the complete being must necesarily be steadfast in the knowledge of the complete being himself, as himself. If he does not have this knowledge, in all likelihood his teaching will make completeness out to be something other than oneself — something which has to be gained by effort. At best, if he is learned in the scriptures he will be able to teach about completeness as indirect knowledge from scriptures, unvalidated by himself.

A teacher who does not know himself teaches from indirect knowledge. He will say things like "the scriptures *tell* us that there is a complete, adequate being hidden within who must be uncovered by the practice of austerities — who will be discovered in the light of meditation". We read such things in books and we also hear them from teachers who have not understood the scriptures and do not know themselves as the complete being.

Such statements mislead the seeker. The complete being can never be covered; it only seems so due to ignorance. Nothing can cover the complete being because it *is* the complete being. Just as space cannot be covered by the things in it, so completeness cannot be covered. Being all-pervasive, space cannot be covered by anything in it. Similarly, the complete being cannot be covered by anything — not by any form of thoughts, memories, tendencies, sins, habits. The only thing that can cover the complete being is ignorance. Just a dash of ignorance can cover the complete being. The complete being can only be covered by not knowing that "I am the complete being". That is all that is required. The whole problem is nothing but ignorance.

Therefore, the wise person, the one who can teach the knowledge, is *brahmaniṣṭham* — who knows very clearly, "I am the complete being". He knows that the complete being is not an object different from himself. Therefore he will not say, "The scriptures say that there is a complete being within you hidden by a variety of things which you must remove..." He will say, "You are the complete being". And because he knows, his words will carry weight. His words can carry no weight if he does not know. To tell you that you are the full, complete being — that you are all-happiness — the teacher must know that he is full, complete — that he is happiness itself. The teacher must be happy for his words to work as a means of knowledge when he tells you that you are full, complete happiness. An unhappy person cannot teach you that you are happiness simply because the scriptures say so.

Inadequate Teaching Can Make the Problem Worse

A teacher who cannot impart the knowledge of completeness to the student — cannot directly teach that the student is the adequate being—either because he does not have command of the methodology to impart what he knows, or because he does not himself know his own nature, can worsen the student's problem. To continue to feel unhappy after one has been told that one is completely adequate — happiness itself — is an infinitely worse situation than thinking that one needs to *do* something to become happy.

Such a situation is like the case of a miserably poor man who discovers that he is the heir to a huge fortune but is too poor to pay the legal fees to establish his claim to the inheritance. The knowledge of the wealth he owns but cannot claim makes him more miserable than before. He feels worse than he did before he knew that he was entitled to the inheritance. To know that the wealth is there, rightfully his, yet have no access to it, creates more problems for him than he earlier had in his simple poverty.

Similarly, to be told that one is complete, adequate without being able to appreciate that completeness makes the misery of the human predicament more acute. That kind of teaching does not really help anyone. It only creates more problems. Therefore, the *Muṇḍaka* verse says:

brahmaniṣṭham gurum abhigacchet

Go to a teacher steadfast in the knowledge of himself as completeness.

Go to a master who can say, convincingly, "That thou art". Unless he sees for himself what he is, the teacher cannot make the statement with conviction to his student. So go to a teacher who is *brahmaniṣṭha,* steadfast in the knowledge of himself.

The Teacher Should Know the Traditional Methodology

The verse also says:

śrotriyaṁ gurum abhigacchet

Go to a teacher learned in the subject matter.

To be learned in the subject matter includes knowledge of the methodology of teaching. A good teacher is one who has learned from his teacher *how* to teach. An established method of teaching is called *sampradāya,* i.e., a traditional handing down of instruction.

So the *guru,* the teacher, should have the *sampradāya,* the methodology for teaching the knowledge of oneself. Because of the peculiarity of the subject matter, for the knowledge of oneself the method of teaching is as important as the subject matter.

When one seeks to know oneself, the situation is not the same as seeking to know an object. An object is something available for demonstration. One or more of the five senses can grasp an object. By definition an object is what is external to the subject, objectifiable by the senses. From infancy onwards, the senses, supported by the mind, are busy objectifying all things in their environment and storing these perceptions in memory; names for many of these perceived objects are also learned. The mother holds out a flower to her baby and pointing to the blossom, says "yellow flower"; then she points to a lemon, "yellow fruit"; later, she shows the child a canary and says, "yellow bird". The child can see the objects; it can see their colour; it can reason that what mother is talking about is their colour, that being what they have in common. From this mind-assisted perception the child learns to call a particular colour perception "yellow". The colour yellow is available for perception.

anu

No particular problem is presented in teaching what is available for perception. However, that is not the case where the subject matter is the nature of oneself. The teacher cannot *show* you the self because what you are seeking to know is not what can be seen with the eye, but is the seer himself. One seeks to know the nature of the observer — not the nature of the observation. So to know oneself presents a very peculiar situation; the subject matter is not available to the usual means of knowledge.

The Teacher must Demolish Wrong Conclusions

The teacher has another problem. Not only is the self not available for objectification but the seeker of self knowledge has usually also reached very definite conclusions about himself; conclusions which get in the way when he tries to understand what the teacher is saying. The student's attitude towards himself makes the teacher's task difficult indeed. The student comes to the teacher with deep-seated convictions about himself. All his life he has struggled to be happy, complete, and free. But, for all his struggles, he still sees himself as weak, inadequate, powerless, lacking. These are well-entrenched conclusions about himself. He has never for a moment had an inkling that he might be complete, full, free from all limitations, that he might be limitlessness itself. If the teacher simply says to such a student, "You are the complete being", the student, sitting there with all his limitations and inhibitions, will not be able to accept that statement, let alone understand it. In fact, he will argue that he is not complete and will bring all the learning at his command, logic, mathematics, physics, sciences, to prove how incomplete he is. To be able to make such a student realize that he is complete, the teacher must have a quick wit and a thorough knowledge of the content and methodology of teaching. He must be prepared to encounter and demolish all possible conditioning and all possible schools of speculative thought. He must be able to remove belief systems not supported by direct discovery (the belief that one is complete is not the same as the knowledge of one's completeness). He must be able to strip words, such as "eternal", of their vagueness and use them in such a way that they convey precisely what he wants them to convey. Such a teacher is called a *śrotriya,* one learned in content and methodology.

Both Self-Knowledge and Methodology are Needed

To be a teacher of the knowledge of the adequate being, it is not just enough to be a *brahmaniṣṭha,* one steadfast in the knowledge that he is the adequate being. The teacher also must be a *śrotriya,* one who knows the methodology. It is like the difference between a singer and a music teacher. To teach music, it is not enough that one knows how to sing. A singer, untrained in the teaching methodology of music may help you follow his example for a few moments, or he may inspire you to seek the knowledge of music, but he cannot make a musician out of you.

Similarly, one who is *brahmaniṣṭha,* nothing more, has solved the basic human quest for himself; he knows himself to be complete; but that by itself does not give him the methodology for helping another to fulfil the quest. He may be a great source of inspiration. His happiness and quietude may be compelling. He can be seen, quiet and simple, his happiness complete, independent of people, possessions, circumstances. People will be attracted to him and their minds, too, may become quieter in his presence. His example may be an inspiration for them. But unless he knows the methodology of teaching he cannot be a source of knowledge for others. For a teacher, therefore, knowledge of the method of teaching is as important as knowledge of the subject matter itself. Otherwise, it becomes mysticism. For mysticism no tradition is required; there may be inspiration, but no methodology; no way for the teacher to communicate the vision to the student.

Teaching should be infallible. When a student goes to a teacher to gain knowledge, the teacher should have a way to communicate that knowledge to the student. Knowledge is about what *is*. Anything that *is*, anything that exists, should be available for disclosure. Knowledge, if it is knowledge, is available for communication. For anything that is available for communication, there can be a teaching tradition. The nature of the object involved in the communication determines the method of communication.

When what is taught is the adequate self, a particular method of communication is needed, on account of the nature of the subject matter. The subject matter being the subject, oneself, a very special method for its teaching is called for. One who teaches it must know the special method, and be an expert in handling it.

The scriptures, *śruti,* clearly state what the nature of one's self is. "You are *brahman*. You are completeness, fullness—the totally adequate being you long to be." If one hears these words from a teacher and still does not know for oneself, "I am *brahman;* I am the complete being", the scriptures are not to be blamed. Śruti, scripture, has not failed. It is the teacher who is to be blamed. The teacher has to make you see that you are *brahman*. Teaching does not consist in the teacher simply repeating, "You are *brahman,*". The teaching must be based on a methodology that makes you see that you are *brahman*.

The words of the scripture say that you are limitlessness—full, complete-beingness; but for you to see that fact the teacher must know the *sampradāya,* know the methodology which creates a context that leads you to see for yourself the fact behind the words. Until you see that fact, the teacher must continue to teach.

The Flow of Knowledge from Teacher to Student

When did it begin, this traditional teaching that reveals the nature of oneself? The teaching flows from teacher to student. Every *guru* who is a *śrotriya* and a *brahmaniṣṭha,* was once a *mumukṣu*. And his teacher also was once a student; and so, too, the teacher before him. Seeking to identify the first teacher is like seeking to identify the first father. We know there was a father because there is a son and every son has a father; and know, too, that the father once was a son. It does not change the example if you protest that once upon a time the father was a monkey. He was still a father. All that can be said is that a father was there because the son is here. The *guru* was there because the teacher is here. Just as my presence here establishes that the parentage leading to me was continuous, similarly the presence of a student taught by a teacher establishes that the teacher-student lineage has never been broken. This is what is called the *guru śisya parampara,* the flow of traditional knowledge handed down from teacher to student.

The Traditional Teaching of Self-Knowledge is Called Vedānta

This traditional teaching, a teaching without a beginning is called Vedānta.

veda	a body of knowledge
anta	end

Vedānta means that which is at the end of the Veda. The Vedas, a body of scriptural knowledge, are four in number—*Ṛg, Yajur, Sāma,* and *Atharva.* The texts found at the end of each of these four vedas deal with the nature of oneself. So in the scriptures known as the Vedas there is a section at the end of each Veda which deals with the nature of self. It is here that knowledge of oneself is unfolded. These sections of the Vedas and their contents, the teaching of knowledge of oneself, are known as Vedānta. The place, the content and the teaching of that content are collectively known as Vedānta.

We do not see the beginning of the teaching. It is just taken back to the *ṛṣis*, the inspired sages to whom the Veda was revealed. We do not bother about the *m ūla*, the root of these sages; *rsi mūlam na vicarayet*, the origin of the *ṛṣis* is not to be questioned. If one must go beyond the *ṛṣis*, then it can just be said the *guru* is the Lord. The same thing is said about the first father—he is the creator, the father of all, the Lord. The first *guru* is the same creator, for it is with the creator that knowledge rests. Any knowledge belongs to the creator. To go beyond the *ṛṣis*, the teaching is traced to the Lord alone—the creator. In fact, the source of any knowledge has to be traced to the creator alone. Upon careful analysis, no knowledge can be traced to any given person—it always leads back to the creator.

So this knowledge of oneself called Vedānta which comes from the creator, which is found at the end of the Veda, which can be traced back to the ancient sages called the *ṛṣis*, passes from teacher to student in the traditional flow of teaching called the *guru-śiṣya-paramparā*. This flow of knowledge, the *guru śiṣya paramparā.*, is revered by the teacher and the student alike because it is an instrument for solving the fundamental human problem. Traditional study generally begins with a tribute to the teaching and to the teachers—to those who focus the light that dispels the ignorance concealing the nature of oneself. Thus one salutes the *guru-śiṣya-paramparā*:

> *Sadāśivasamārambhāṁ*
> *śaṅkarācāryamadhyamām*
> *asmadācāryaparyantāṁ*
> *vande guruparamparām*

Beginning auspiciously with the Lord, with the teacher, Śaṅkara, in the middle, extending as far as my teacher, I salute progression of teachers.

CHAPTER SIX

The Text

The Two Sections of the Veda

Vedānta is a body of teaching found at the end of the Veda. The vedas, four in number, *Ṛg*, *Yajur*, *Sāma*, and *Atharva*, are each divided into two sections. The first section deals with *dharma*, religious ethics; *karma*, religious actions, various rituals; *artha*, other special actions to achieve security; and *kāma* pleasures. This section, called the *karmakāṇḍa*, the "action section", is very bulky, understandably so, because it deals with human desires and the actions needed to fulfil the desires. Human desires are many; to detail the variety of means, called *karma*, required to secure their fulfilment does require much space.

The last section of the Veda is called *jñānakāṇḍa*, the "knowledge section". It is a very much shorter section because its subject matter is a single desire *mokṣa* the desire for liberation. The fulfilment of that desire is not through actions, which are many, but through knowledge, which is singular with regard to the particular thing to be known.

The ways of knowing a particular thing are not many, for these have to be the particular, appropriate means determined by the nature of what is to be known. Thus, the second section of the vedas, the "knowledge section", called Vedānta, is a short one.

The Variety of Action

When the means to achieve a given end is action, *karma*, there can always be some choice. There are many ways of doing and achieving the same thing. **About action it is said:**

Kartuṁ śakyam	Onc can do it.
akartuṁ śakyam	One can not do it.
anyathā vā kartuṁ śakyam	One can do it differently.
Example: Jim, come here!	Jim is able to come. Jim is not able to come. Jim is able to come in his own way (jumping, skipping, running, walking, now, later).

Thus, for an end that has to be achieved through effort there is a variety of possible actions, *karma*, to choose as a means for that end.

Every individual has many desires. The individuals who entertain these desires too, are many. Desires vary from individual to individual, and from time to time within an individual; these variations are many. The possible actions, *karma*, which will achieve these various desires are also many and varied. Therefore, the *karmakāṇḍa*, the first part of the Veda, dealing with actions that achieve desires, is truly a vast one.

The Role of Scriptures

Veda, meaning "knowledge", is the name for the body of Indian scriptural knowledge. A scripture is a body of knowledge considered divinely authoritative, about matters which cannot be known by the ordinary means of knowledge.

The Veda, both the first and the second sections, for the most part are a means of knowledge for things which one cannot come to know by one's inherent means of knowledge—the five senses supported by the mind.

Knowledge of the Subtle Results of Action

The *karmakāṇḍa* is the source of knowledge of the special religious actions—rituals, prayers, meditations needed for gaining of security and pleasure in this world and hereafter. It is also the section where religious ethics are detailed. As we have seen, religious ethics codify commonsense ethics, based on the way one wants to be treated by others, and add something more. The "something more" which is added is the idea of *puṇya* and *pāpa,* merit and demerit, which accrue to the performer of actions.

Puṇya, merit, is the subtle result of a good action. *Pāpa,* demerit, is the subtle result of a bad action. Commonsense ethics as codified in the rules of *dharma* and *adharma* give the standards for determining whether an action is "good" or "bad". The subtle result of a good action is *puṇya,*, the occurrence of an enjoyable, pleasant experience at some later time. The subtle result of a bad action is *pāpa,* an uncomfortable or painful experience at a later time. If one refuses to be sad, all *pāpa,* can do is give some physical pain. If you accept discomfort, then *pāpa,* can do nothing to you. You cannot be touched by an external situation which is the negative result of past actions if you are insulated against any kind of reaction to it. Maturity of thinking gives that insulation. Generally, man is not so insulated. He wants to be comfortable in all ways; therefore, *pāpa,* the uncomfortable subtle result of an adharmic action, is to be avoided. *Puṇya,* the pleasant, comfortable result of a dharmic action is to be sought.

Knowledge of Heaven

The pleasurable rewards of *puṇya,* are often reserved for heaven. The rituals and other kinds of action that will take one to heaven are set out in the first section of the Veda. Heaven is viewed as something of a temporary holiday home. It is a place that one enters and leaves later. Thus, heavenly life is not eternal. It has a beginning. What begins is not eternal. Anything you can enter you can also leave. What is eternal is always present. The *karmakāṇḍa* section of the Veda tells how to reach heaven. There are many ways, some of which seem contradictory. You can gain heaven by charitable actions, by dying in battle, by winning in battle, by certain rituals, by prayers, by good actions, and so forth. There are always many ways to accomplish that which is gained by action. Thus, there are many ways to reach heaven. These ways are pointed out in the first section of the Veda.

Why does one want to go to heaven? Because it promises what one misses here on earth. It is said that in heaven one will have an adult but youthful body; all the objects of pleasure will be freely available. In heaven, one suffers no denial of pleasure for want of the object or want of an adequate instrument for its enjoyment. This pleasurable condition remains constant so long as one is in heaven. One does not age, nor do one's circumstances change from the pleasant to the unpleasant. This is the picture of heaven that the Veda gives. One has no data to prove or disprove this account of heaven. Therefore, one's conviction that this account is either true or untrue, must rest on belief or disbelief alone.

The Veda also tell us that heaven is not a place where one performs actions, *karma,* that accrue good or bad subtle results. One is not a performer of action in heaven, only an enjoyer. Heaven, then, is a holiday experience, like a trip to Hawaii. One goes there just to spend money and enjoy oneself for a while. On a vacation trip one does not earn — one only spends. It is only in a place like earth where one has a human body that one both "sows and reaps" — enjoys the results of past actions and creates more subtle results to be experienced at a later time. Such an earth-like place is called a *karma-bhūmi*, a place for performing action.

So, in heaven, one only enjoys, spending the previously earned capital — *puṇya*; in heaven one acquires no new capital. When all one's *puṇya* has been exhausted, one then leaves heaven.

The Bhagavadgītā says:

te taṁ bhuktvā svargalokaṁ viśālam
kṣīṇe puṇya, martyalokaṁ viśanti
evaṁ trayīdharmam anuprapannāḥ
gatāgataṁ kāmakāmā labhante

Bhagavadgītā, IX, 21

Having enjoyed the spacious world of heaven, *puṇya*, exhausted, they enter the world of mortals, thus, carrying out the mandate of the three Vedas. Desiring objects of desire, they gain going and coming.

Having enjoyed the heavenly abode, when the *puṇya*, capital is spent, one comes back to the earth.

So one of the subjects that the *karma-kaṇḍa* section of the Veda deals with is how to achieve heaven. But it should be well understood that achieving heaven, even if one believes it to be available, is but a pleasurable respite. It is non-eternal. It does not give freedom from limitedness. In heaven there are many inhabitants. Some have earned better bodies than others. Some are entitled to sweeter pleasures. There are degrees of enjoyment. And, finally, the period of enjoyment always come to an end.

Heaven, then is not liberation. Heaven is achieved through actions, *karma*. There is no liberation through *karma*.

The Knowledge of Rituals

In addition to the gain of heaven, the *karmakāṇḍa* contains an account of many other ends which can be gained through various religious actions. Certain rituals are performed to produce desired results. There are two categories of rituals for the purpose of obtaining results: (1) those that will produce results right away; and (2) others that will produce results later.

Both types of rituals are called *karma*, those which produce results now and those which produce results later. Because there are rituals prescribed which will produce results immediately, here, in this life itself, there is a way to test whether or not these Vedic *karma* work: perform the ritual and see what happens.

The rituals of the Veda do seem to work. There are, for example, rituals for producing rain. You can have such a ritual performed and see whether or not it rains. A few years ago an American professor carried out this test. He was a professor of Eastern Studies in an American university and he wanted to subject the Vedic *karma* he had studied to a real test. He went to Kerala where he collected a group of scholars and asked them to perform such a ritual. He paid the substantial sum of money which was required for the ritual. It was the time of year when no rain could be expected and no clouds or any evidence of any kind indicated that it might rain. The ritual was performed on a dry, bright, cloudless day. Just as the last ceremony necessary to complete the ritual was performed the sky became clouded and the rains came — in great abundance. So much rain fell that the ritual could not actually be completed. So it would seem that the rituals really work. If the rituals performed for immediate results work when tested, then we can assume that those aimed at results in the future, or in worlds hereafter, may work as well.

"How-to" Knowledge is not an End in Itself

So the first section of the Veda contains the knowledge of how to do a variety of actions which can produce given results now or later. This scriptural "how to" knowledge is a knowledge not found elsewhere. The knowledge itself does not produce the desired result, but tells us how to do the actions that will produce the results. The mere knowledge of action is not an end in itself. Anything to be achieved in time depends upon effort. Knowledge of the special efforts that achieve a chosen end is necessary to gain that end; but that knowledge is not the end itself. Knowledge does not gain the end. Action gains the end. Knowledge tells what actions to perform.

For example: If I am hungry and need to eat, certain knowledge is important to me: the knowledge of what things are edible; the knowledge of where to find such things; and the knowledge of how to prepare and cook them. The knowledge of all the *karmas*, all the actions, does not appease my hunger. Only doing the actions, and making the final necessary effort, the action of eating, is what appeases my hunger.

Thus the knowledge found in the *karma-kāṇḍa* section of the Veda is not an end in itself. This knowledge reveals which action needs to be done to gain the desired end. This is true of *dharma* as well. The knowledge of the many religious ethical values, *dharma*, found in the first section of the Veda, is not an end in itself. A life of *dharma* is followed in accordance with the rules set forth to avoid pain. No one likes *duḥkha*, sorrow, pain; everyone wants *sukha*, happy experiences. Therefore the "do's and don'ts" set forth in the first section of the Veda are important to all those who seek to extract more *sukha* than *duḥkha* from a life centred on action. But mere knowledge, of all the "do's and don'ts" does not result in the gain of *sukha*-producing *puṇya*, or the avoidance of *duḥkha*-producing *pāpa*. The knowledge of the ethics called *dharma* must be put into practice through action in order to earn a favorable or unfavorable subtle result. All *dharma* (the ethical mandates) are meant for *karma*, action. Mere knowledge of ethics is not going to help. Knowledge of truthfulness does not make one truthful. Ethics must be expressed in action.

Mere knowledge is not an end in itself when what has to be gained is something not-yet-achieved in time or space. The gain of the not-yet-achieved requires effort. Knowledge of which efforts are appropriate, and how to perform them is helpful but does not produce the result. The knowledge must be put into practice through action. Knowledge of heaven is not an end in itself; the gaining of heaven is the end. Knowledge of how to get to heaven must be put into practice through action.

Knowledge as an End in Itself

On the other hand, if what is desired to be achieved is already an accomplished but unrecognized fact, then knowledge is an end in itself. This is the kind of knowledge that is the subject matter of the *jñānakāṇḍa*, the second section of the Veda, called Vedānta. This section deals with the adequate, limitless self that everyone wants to be. If the adequate, limitless self is my nature, unrecognized by me, then knowledge of that fact makes me the gainer of what I seek. Knowledge and the end are identical when what one wants to gain is already a gained fact.

Both sections of the Veda are sources of knowledge about things for which one has no other means of knowledge. But the role of knowledge in each section is different. In the first section there is knowledge about a variety of actions which are to be done to gain a variety of unrealized ends. The second section contains knowledge about a single, already-achieved but unrecognized end which is gained through the knowledge itself: gain of the knowledge is gain of the end.

Special Name for End of the Veda Justified

At first, it may seem unnecessary to specially distinguish a small section at the end of the Veda with the separate name, Vedānta. But when it is seen how much the two sections differ, a separate name is justified. True to the general purpose of scriptures, both sections reveal something that one cannot know through some other means of knowledge. But here their similarity ends. The two sections are clearly distinguishable from each other as to their subject matter, purpose, method, and intended audience.

The first section deals with knowledge meant to be put into practice — acted upon to fulfil its purpose. It is the knowledge of certain actions and results. Actions and results are always many, everchanging, limited in nature. None is constant; none is without limitation. The audience for this section are those who are seeking security and happiness through action. They seek through the gain of security and pleasures (in this life or the next) to escape all insufficiency — to find completeness. They have not yet realized that no amount of gain solves the problem of feeling incomplete.

The second section, Vedānta., deals with knowledge that does not have to be put into practice. It is the end itself. This is the knowledge of the completely adequate being — the *vastu*, that which is real, unchanging, without limitation.

The Student of the Karmakāṇḍa

The first section of the Veda serves those who have not yet identified the problem. The "how to" knowledge of the *karmakāṇḍa* is useful for the *avivekī*, the person who is undiscriminating in that he has not really discerned the basic human problem. It is meant for the person who is seeking — here or in another world — limited objectives achievable through action. It is for the one who seeks rain, wealth, health, power, progeny, pleasures, and comforts, the gain of heaven, and the avoidance of hell. The student of this section may gain some pleasure and comfort from his pursuits but remains a deficient person. The knowledge found here is not an end itself but enables one to perform the action that gains the end. The end gained is always a limited result.

The Student of Vedānta

Vedānta, the second section of the Veda, serves those who have discovered the problem. This section is for the *vivekī*, the person with discrimination who understands the basic human problem and who knows that *dharma, artha,* and *kāma*, ethics, security and pleasures—cannot solve that problem.

From the analysis of his own experiences the *vivekī* has discerned his fundamental problem: "Most of the time I seem to be a limited, inadequate being but what I long to be is the limitless, complete being that occasionally I seem to be."

The *vivekī* understands that the limitlessness which he seeks can only be gained through knowledge, not by any kind of action. He has seen that behind all his striving to gain unaccomplished goals (for which how-to knowledge plus action are the means) there is a basic goal which cannot be gained through action: completeness. Completeness, by its very nature, cannot be a goal which is *aprāptasya prāpti,* not-yet-achieved, a limited goal achievable by limited actions. Completeness can only be a goal which is *prāptasya prāpti,* already-achieved, but not recognized; a goal for the gain of which knowledge alone is all that is required.

The kind of person drawn to the study of Vedānta is one who, having discovered that actions being limited cannot produce what he wants, has gained a certain dispassion towards action and results. Naturally, then, a *vivekī* is also in some measure dispassionate toward worldly pursuits, *a vairāgī*. He is the informed seeker who has come to appreciate that *dharma* and *karma*, are not the means for freedom from limitation. It is not enough simply to live a clean, ethical life. Actions, no matter how ethical, cannot produce liberation. *Mokṣa* is not gained through *dharma*. Pleasant but limited experiences can be gained through *dharma*. A state of mind that is quiet and open to knowledge can also be gained through *dharma*. But liberation comes only through knowledge, not through any kind of action.

It is this knowledge, the knowledge of one's own nature, that the student of Vedānta is seeking. And it is this knowledge, the knowledge that is both the means and the end — the knowledge that solves the fundamental human problem — that, found as it is at the end of the Veda, is known as Vedānta.

The student of Vedānta seeks knowledge which will reveal to him his own true nature, reveal whether he is by nature limited or whether he is limitlessness. For this he needs a special source of knowledge. The knowledge here is the end itself. It is knowledge like the "teaching" of the old man in the story of the Tenth Man. When the old man told the grieving leader, "You are the tenth man", the leader did not have to do anything to obtain the tenth man. The knowledge itself "delivered" the tenth man. Similarly, when what one seeks is freedom from limitation, the very unfoldment and discovery of the nature of oneself is the end. No action, no "practice" is required to implement the discovery.

Words Are Means of Knowledge in Both Sections of the Veda

In both sections of the Veda, words are the means of knowledge about matters for which we have no other means available. We have seen earlier how words can give both indirect and direct knowledge. Words give indirect knowledge when the object to be known is away from one in space or time. When the words in the first section of the Veda are giving knowledge about something like *puṇya*, and *pāpa*, or heaven and hell, the knowledge is indirect. The objects of such knowledge are not available for immediate appreciation. Verbal knowledge about things not immediately available for appreciation — about things separated from one in time or space — is indirect knowledge.

Words give direct knowledge when the object of knowledge is immediately available for appreciation. The object of knowledge of the second section of the Veda, of Vedānta, is oneself. What kind of knowledge — direct or indirect — can words give to one about oneself?

The Words of Vedānta Give Direct Knowledge of Oneself

What kind of knowledge can be gained from words about that "I" who is the seeker, the struggler, the seer, hearer, smeller, taster, toucher, walker, worker — that "I", who is confused about its own nature? Words can give direct knowledge. I am always here, immediately available. I am never away from myself. I am not remote in the sense that heaven is remote. I am very much here experiencing myself. I experience myself as a sad person, an incomplete person. Occasionally, I experience myself as a happy, full person. I am always immediately available to myself. In fact, I am the only thing which is directly experienced all the time. My experience of all things depends upon me being here, available to experience the "others". My experience of everything else is dependent upon my means of knowledge, upon my cognition, my thinking. My knowledge that the sun is in the sky overhead, that a cool wind blows, that a rock blocks my path, is dependent upon exercising my means of knowledge — my senses, assisted by my mind, the receiver of that sense data. Objects do not announce themselves to me. They do not prove themselves to me. Their existence is proved only when I use my means of knowledge.

However, I am self-proven. I do not have to apply my means of knowledge to know that I am here. I am always here. To be able to see, hear, taste, smell, and think, I must already be here. Before seeing, before hearing, before thinking, I am already here as a person. I, who use the means of knowledge for knowing objects other than myself, can never be a remote object. I am always here. Therefore, I am always available for direct knowledge of myself.

It is not possible for me to be an object of indirect knowledge. I can never gain indirect knowledge of something that is now being experienced by me. If the knowledge I gain of myself is valid it will be direct knowledge, which my experience immediately corroborates.

The only knowledge which I can gain about myself through words will be direct knowledge. The knowledge that words can give me about myself will either be the direct knowledge that I am a complete person or the direct knowledge that I am an incomplete being. There can never be indirect knowledge about oneself. It is very important to understand this clearly. For only when this is understood is one truly ready for the teaching of Vedānta.

From the teaching of Vedānta, the teaching of the knowledge of myself, I shall gain either the direct, immediate knowledge that I am a complete, full person, lacking nothing, or I shall gain the direct immediate, knowledge that I am an incomplete, deficient person. Words will give me either direct knowledge about myself or no knowledge at all.

Handling the Words of Vedānta

Like any instrument of knowledge, words must be handled appropriately under the right conditions so that they give valid knowledge of the object. For eyes to work, there must be enough light. For some eyes, corrective lenses are required. For ears to discriminate a given sound, there must be the right volume, the right distance, and the right notes. For the nose to work, there must be no blockage from a cold. For the words of Vedānta to work as an instrument of knowledge, they must be properly heard from a teacher who, knowing the methodology, can make the words deliver the knowledge of oneself. Words unfolded in a particular context — used in accordance with a particular methodology — are the means of knowing oneself.

As a means of knowledge, the words of Vedānta have a very special kind of job to do. The vision of Vedānta is that one is the complete, full being, lacking nothing — that one's nature is limitlessness itself. This vision must be imparted as direct knowledge (the self being immediately available for knowing) through words. But words, themselves, are limited in nature. Moreover, from person to person the significance of words varies. The teacher, thus, has the task of revealing something limitless by a limited means, words, and to choose and handle these words so that he is able to communicate exactly what he wants to communicate. The words he uses must be known to the student, and he must beware of defining unknown words with more unknown words. When the meaning of "immortal" is unknown, it does not help to define it as "eternal", another word whose meaning is equally unclear. So the teacher avoids fuzzy words like "eternal", "supreme", "spiritual", the meanings of which are really unknown to the student. The teacher of Vedānta uses ordinary, known words. But he creates a context which enables these words, limited though they be, to make the student see his limitlessness.

It is this imperative of creating a context which makes the teacher so important. The teacher must know the methodology which enables him to create the context in which the words can show one one's limitlessness. In such a context a student with a mind which is prepared and open to the words of the teaching, comes to see the nature of himself.

The Mind Must be Attentive

All means of knowledge have one condition in common which must be met so that they may work. That common condition is the possession of the full attention of the mind.

The mind must support the operative means of knowledge. It must be alert so that the eyes can see, the ears can hear, the nose can smell, the tongue can taste, and the hand can feel. The food may be upon the tongue but if the mind is riveted elsewhere it will not register any taste.

The same is true for the other sense organs. The sound may be loud but the ears do not hear it if the mind is absorbed in something else. The eyes may be wide open but nothing will be seen if the mind is busy daydreaming. The sense organs can operate properly only when they are supported by a mind which is not otherwise occupied or distracted by reactions, emotions, fears and prejudices which can interfere with clear perception. Knowledge is the appreciation of what is. Therefore, valid perception must be just as the object is. The mind must not be a vitiating factor in perception. It must be fresh, open, attentive—available for the perception of just what is.

Similarly, for the words of Vedānta to act as a means of knowledge, the mind should be fresh, non-interfering and non-vitiating: a simple, clean mind is required for the words to have their proper result. For both, the operation of a sense organ and the exposure to words, the mind must surrender to the means of knowledge if it is to perform its function. When the knowledge is a perception, the mind must surrender at the altar of the sense organ, so that the perception can be true to the object perceived. The same holds good when the means of knowledge is the spoken word coming from a teacher. The mind must be behind the ears to hear the sounds that are the words and also behind the words to see their meaning. This is what is meant by "surrender to the words of the teaching".

The words of Vedānta are themselves the means of knowledge not an aid to some other means. Just as eyes are not an aid to seeing but are the means by which one sees, so, too, the words of Vedānta are not an aid to knowing oneself but are the very means by which one knows oneself. Vedānta is not an aid which makes it *easier* to understand the nature of oneself through some other means. Vedānta *is* the means. The words of Vedānta *are* the instrument for knowing oneself just as the eye is the instrument for seeing. Thus as the mind must surrender to the eye for vision to take place, so must the mind surrender to the words of Vedānta for knowledge of oneself. And, surrendering to the words of Vedānta simply means having an attentive mind which can clearly hear the words that are spoken and grasp their meaning.

The Proof of Vedānta

How can it be proved that the words of Vedānta indeed give direct knowledge of oneself? Listen first, to this story of the man who was born blind.

A certain man was born totally blind. He was unable to see form and colour or distinguish light from darkness. The condition of his sight did not change as he grew to manhood. He became an adult whose world was limited to that which could be objectified by his four good sense organs. However, there came a day when his doctor advised him that there was now a surgical procedure which could perhaps enable him to see. Sponsored by a local charitable club, the blind man flew off to a large metropolitan hospital where a specialist performed the operation. For several days afterwards, he was bandaged and blindfolded to allow the healing to take place. Finally, the day came when the doctor very carefully removed the bandages, and then said, "Please, open your eyes".

The patient, keeping his eyes tightly shut, replied "Please guarantee me that I will be able to see—only then will I open my eyes".

"I assure you, you will see. The operation was a success. Please open your eyes."

"No, no. After all these years, I do not want to be disappointed. I do not want the shock of that. Prove to me first that I will see, then alone shall I open my eyes. Otherwise, I do not want to take a chance on such a disappointing experience."

What can the doctor do? Nothing. There is nothing he can say or do to prove that the formerly blind eyes are not cured. The proof lies only in the opening of the eyes. The eyes must be opened to find out if they see. That alone is the proof. There is none other. The eyes alone are the means of knowledge of sight.

Any means of knowledge is self-proving. It is not something that is proven by another means of knowledge. If it is said that the words of Vedānta are a means of knowledge for knowing oneself, then the only proof of this statement is to test those words and see whether they work.

When it is said that the words of Vedānta reveal the nature of yourself and, that in the vision of Vedānta you are not the inadequate self you think yourself to be—you are the self that is free from all limitations—you must necessarily give yourself an exposure to the teaching. For that is their only proof: you must see for yourself whether they work or not.

By creating a context the teacher removes the inherent limitations of words to make you see the limitlessness that you are. The open, attentive mind begins to see the meaning of the words, grasp their magical message, as they reveal oneself to be the complete, full being lacking nothing, limitlessness itself.